Cumbria
Edited by Donna Samworth

 Young**Writers**

First published in Great Britain in 2008 by:
Young Writers
Remus House
Coltsfoot Drive
Peterborough
PE2 9JX
Telephone: 01733 890066
Website: www.youngwriters.co.uk

SB ISBN 978-1 84431 629 8

Foreword

Young Writers was established in 1991 and has been passionately devoted to the promotion of reading and writing in children and young adults ever since. The quest continues today. Young Writers remains as committed to the nurturing of poetic and literary talent as ever.

This year's Young Writers competition has proven as vibrant and dynamic as ever and we are delighted to present a showcase of the best poetry from across the UK and in some cases overseas. Each poem has been selected from a wealth of *Little Laureates 2008* entries before ultimately being published in this, our seventeenth primary school poetry series.

Once again, we have been supremely impressed by the overall quality of the entries we have received. The imagination, energy and creativity which has gone into each young writer's entry made choosing the poems a challenging and often difficult but ultimately hugely rewarding task - the general high standard of the work submitted ensured this opportunity to bring their poetry to a larger appreciative audience.

We sincerely hope you are pleased with this final collection and that you will enjoy *Little Laureates 2008 Cumbria* for many years to come.

Contents

Austin Friars St Monica's Junior School

Katie Robinson (8) 1
Sofia Feghali (7) 1
William Martyn Ewart (8) 1
Joseph Waterfield (7) 1
Rafe Houston (7) 2
Edward Anthony Mullock (8) 2
Samuel Wilson (7) 2
Courtney Reynolds (7) 2
Isabella Mullock (8) 3
Ellie Graham (7) 3
Alyshia Gill (7) 3
Gregor Ian Gilchrist (7) 3
Bryony Temple (8) 4
Eve White (8) 4
Eve Elise Jamieson (7) 4
Olivia Jane Fisher (7) 4
Harrington Moore (9) 5
Gayathri Nair (8) 5
Jodi Wilkinson (7) 5
Jessie Brown (7) 5
Jane Irving (8) 6
John Colwell (9) 6
Ailsa Duncan (8) 6
Bruce Long (9) 7
Sarah Margaret Long (8) 7
Thomas Harrison (9) 7
Isabel Leitch (9) 8
Joseph Logue (9) 8
Adrian Anderson (8) 8
William Ferdinand (9) 9
Rory Sutton (9) 9
Daniel Lumb (9) 9
Harry Blowing (9) 10
Rupert Rosindell (9) 10
Molly Pattinson (8) 10
Niccolo Vetta (9) 11
Kathryn Orr (9) 11
Arron Francis (9) 11

Joy Brouillard (10)	12
Ho Yu Liu (9)	12
Chay Tuuer-Richards (10)	13
Cameron Gilchrist (9)	13
Tara Houston (9)	14
Blair Douglas (10)	14
Robbie Ewart (9)	15
Gemma Stacey (11)	15
Charlie Graham (9)	16
Logan Davidson (10)	16
Victoria Race (10)	17
James Main (10)	17
Polly Mattock (10)	18
John Long (11)	18
Kimberly Bennett (10)	19
Jack Freshwater (11)	19
Hannah McMillan (10)	20
Alice Tod (11)	20
Edwin Wilson (9)	21
William Stonebridge (11)	21
Chloe Isla Thomson (10)	22

Beetham CE Primary School

Laura Maden (9)	22
Ryan Williamson (8)	23
Sam Maden (7)	23
Annalise Harry (9)	24
Ella Handy (8)	25

Belle Vue Junior School

Dylan Beaty (8)	25
Callum Currie (8)	26
Abigail Box (8)	26
Kevan Coady (7)	26
Ellis Dickinson (7)	27
Robert Dalgliesh (7)	27
Joe Dawson (8)	27
Jamie Graham (7)	28
Bailey Gregan (7)	28
Matthew Elliott (7)	28
Sarah Irving (8)	29

Megan Halliburton (7)	29
Richard Hope (8)	29
Ellie Johnson (7)	30
Adam Lofthouse (7)	30
Lewis Jamieson (8)	30
Rosie Steele (8)	31
Jonathan Peacock (7)	31
Patrick Moore (8)	31
Karl Gibson (8)	32
Amber Surtees (8)	32
Brooke Stephenson (7)	32
Ben Walker (8)	33
Lewis Young (8)	33
Reece McLaughlin (10)	33
Jamie Ruddick (7)	34
Ben Lancaster (7)	34
Jasmine Heaton (7)	35
Nathan Halliburton (8)	35
Jordan Armstrong (8)	36
Katie McGarr (7)	36
Catherine Brown (7)	37
Robbie Bell (7)	37
Mark Palmer (8)	38
Austin McVittie (7)	38
Samuel Simpson (8)	39
Harry Caven (8)	39
Brodie Stephenson (7)	40
Oliver Morley (8)	40
Harrison Edgar (8)	41
Bethany Rutherford (8)	41
Megan Abba (8)	42
Rebecca Connor (7)	42
Lewis Dock (7)	42
Sophie Todd (8)	43
Leah Osgood (7)	43
James Hadden (10)	43
James Nixon (10)	44
Rebecca Heyworth (10)	44
Liam Dawson (10)	45
Mark Lofthouse (10)	45
Connor McLaughlin (10)	46
Cameron Keal (10)	46

Chloe Little (10)   46
Megan Fisher (10)   47
Sam Abba (10)   47
Susanna Whiffen (9)   47
Lewis Harkins (11)   48
Charlotte Harty (11)   48
Owen Dowie (10)   48
Joseph Coates (11)   49
Robbie Morley (11)   49
Sophie Armstrong (11)   49
Anna Robbins (11)   50
Jamie Blair (11)   50
Daniel Veitch (10)   50
Ellen Johnston (11)   51
Samantha Graham (10)   51
Becky Osgood (11)   51
Poppy Cutherbertson (9)   52
Lauren Montgomery (10)   52
Joseph Harrison (9)   53
Molly Giles (11)   53
Lauryn Jamieson (10)   54
Aaran Atkinson (9)   54
Jamie Bradley (9)   54
Chelsea Cairns (9)   55
Liam Short (9)   55
Mark Donnelly (9)   55
Oliver Bellingham (9)   56
Hannah-Mae Graham (9)   56
Nicole Atkinson (9)   57
Chloe Notman (9)   57
Emma Bradley (9)   58
Sophie Earl (9)   58
Syd Harty (9)   58
Charlotte Norman (9)   59
Joseph Robson (9)   59
Shaun Lester (9)   59
Niall Sanderson (9)   60
Matthew Story (9)   60
Caitlin Thomson (8)   60
Orla Giles (8)   61
Rebecca Graham (8)   61
Anna Ostridge (8)   61

Caitlin Humes (8)	62
Jacob Bie (8)	62
Sophie Parker (9)	62
Beth Giles (8)	63
Ethan Skowronek (8)	63
Thomas Wilson (9)	63
Lucy Jackson (8)	64
Hollie Notman (8)	64
Matthew Segal (8)	64
April Coward (8)	65
Matthew Ogilvie (9)	65
Jonathon Veitch (8)	65
Holly Aitchison (9)	66
Katie Keal (8)	66
Abbie McLaughlin (9)	66
Georgia Palmer (9)	67
Beth Bannister (9)	67
Emily Frith (8)	68
Victoria Boaden (8)	68
Isabel Harkins (9)	69
Thomas Blythe (10)	69
Sean Campbell (10)	70
Emily Wiggett (10)	70
Maegan Witherington (10)	70
James Lewis Litherland (11)	71
Chloe Kerr (10)	71
Lucy Thompson (10)	72
Liam Farish (11)	72
Jack Lennon (10)	73
Luke Surtees (11)	73

Blue Gate Montessori School, Carlisle

Skye Wohl, Sam Bailey, Teddy Birkbeck, & Oona Roberts (3), Elizabeth Joyce, Francis Peers, Amelie Marshall Jane Mieras (4), Danny Poland (6), & Raf Appleby	74

Braithwaite CE (VA) Primary School

Emily Speck (9)	75
Natalie Field (8)	75
Amy Oxley (9)	76
Timmy Price (9)	76

Alex Halsall (7)	77
Robert Saxton (8)	77
Jasmine Stubbs (8)	78
Bethany Mawdsley (8)	78
Esther Tonkin (8)	79

Eaglesfield Paddle CE (VA) Primary School

Adam Kirkwood (10)	79
Jonathan Magrath (10)	80
Lucy Pye (8)	80
Ella Fanthorpe (10)	81
Matthew Conway (7)	81
Sophie Douglas (7)	82
Rhys Kirkwood (7)	82
Isy Drimmie (8)	83
Ella McGonigle (8)	83
Ciaran Ogilvie (7)	83
Dominique Cowley (8)	84
Chloe Keenan-Wilson (7)	84
Daniel Vives Lynch (7)	84
Matthew Shepherd (8)	85
Keenan McDonald (8)	85
Lucy Hammond (7)	85
Katy Livesey (7)	86
Abbie Louise Caine (8)	86
Harry Davies (8)	86
Ewan Roberts (7)	87
Isla Campbell (8)	87
Adam Bainbridge (7)	87
Roisin Kingsbury (7)	88
Christie Potts (7)	88
Kirsty Jayne Walker (7)	88
Alannah Hambley (7)	89
Jordan Martin (8)	89

Heversham St Peter's CE Primary School

Archie Phillips (8)	89
Francesca Ely (10)	90
Brendan Procter (10)	91
Elliot Handley (9)	91
Didi Davies (10)	92

James Richards (9)	93
Megan Carling (11)	94
Edward Pickthall (10)	94
Ellie Taylor (9)	95
Benedict Willacy (10)	95
Will Jacques (10)	96
Charlotte Haddow (9)	97
Geroge Pickthall (10)	98
Nina Duxbury (10)	99
Ritchie Budd (10)	99
Abbie Thornley (7)	100
Holly Watson (11)	100
Bethany Clare (8)	101
Rachel Nield (10)	101
Megan Thornley (9)	102
Isabel Nield (8)	102
Sophie Watson (9)	102
Brendan McQue (8)	103
Lauren Peers (9)	103
Olivia Budd (9)	104
Callum Cushnie (9)	104
George Duxbury (8)	105
Thomas Moses (8)	105
Jody Tideswell (7)	106
Tom Taylor (8)	106
Rob Calland (9)	107
Hannah Douthwaite (8)	107
Joshua Rushton (8)	108
John Hodgkinson (9)	109
Daniel Dixon (8)	110
Trudi Beuzeval (9)	110
Dennis Dixon (8)	110
Ben Heseltine (7)	111
Oliver Somers (9)	111
Adam Lynch (8)	111
Cameron Blood (9)	112

Holy Family Catholic School

Georgia Cooper (8)	112
Anna Roberts (8)	113
Elizabeth Morgan (8)	113

Emily Russell (7)   114
Tamsyn Duff (7)   115
Jacob McSweeney (7)   115
Jennifer Singleton (7)   116
Lewis Singleton (7)   116
Tommy Robertson (8)   116
Sophie Edmondson (8)   117
William Martin (8)   117
Hannah Alarakia-Charles (7)   117
Sophie Shannon (7)   118
Amy Simpson (8)   118
Maria Guselli (8)   118
Alfie Murphy (8)   119
Morgan Hulston (8)   119

Orton CE School

Lisa Holme (11)   120
Bethany Woof (11)   120
Charlotte Whitham (10)   121
Courtney Wearmouth (11)   121
Tessa Ellen Higgs (11)   122
Emma Elizabeth Barker (10)   122
Jenny Coates (10)   123
Mark Potter (10)   123
Emily Pinder (9)   124
George Mason (10)   124
Keenan Bentley-Todd   125
Harry Laidlow (11)   125

Roose Primary School

Catherine Gorry-Edwards (9)   126
Samuel McDonald (9)   126
Jake Carter (9)   127
Joshua Singleton (8)   127
Amelia Bird (8)   127
Joe McCormick   (8)   128
Chloe Barrow (8)   128
Joshua Woodend (9)   129
Matthew Tongue (9)   129
Francesca Barry (8)   130

Rosley CE Primary School

Jenny Rothery (10)	130
Owen Cundall (9)	131
Rosie Groves (10)	131
Guy Rodger (10)	132

St Joseph's Catholic Primary School, Cockermouth

Benedict Shackleford, Timothy Dixon, Kayley Sharp, Andalucia Armstrong-Squires, Bernadette Thompson, Shay Tinnion (9) & Annie Rebecca Gardner (8)	132
Anna Helen Heywood (11)	133
Kai Cartwright (10)	133
Jonathan Peter Broad (10)	134
Jacinta Ryan (10)	135
Daniel Curry (9)	136
Eweline Zmuda (9)	137
Lauren Sian Coulson (8)	138
Charlotte Gardner (10)	138
Edward Meek	139
Athie Armstrong-Squires (10)	139

Staveley Primary School

Sam Styan (8)	140
Eddy Hubble (7)	140
Adam Baker-Ellwood (7)	141
Oliver Jackson (7)	141
Kieran Raven (8)	141
Robyn Bowness (7)	142
Joanne Smith (7)	143
Millie Whitehead (8)	143
Oliver Clegg (8)	144
Isabel Cambray (8)	144
Jakob Stove (7)	144
Daisy Barker (7)	145
Caleb McLellan (8)	145
Joseph Skelding (8)	145
Jessica Black (7)	146
Amy Wood (8)	146

Windermere Junior School

Calum Davison-Bowden (9)	146
William Crisp (10)	147
Emerson Doore (8)	147
Chloe Ackers (10)	148
Anna McVey (9)	148
Jessica Irwin (11)	149
Rebekah Booth (11)	149
Hannah Thomas (8)	150
Bridey Callingham (11)	151
Ellie-Cesca Williams (8)	151
Colleen Sheehan (11)	152
Mhairi Callingham (9)	152
Rory Noon (10)	153
Luke Williams (9)	153
Chelsea Louise Walker (11)	153
Hannah Clark (11)	154
Jennifer Holden (10)	154
Yasmin Wright (10)	154

The Poems

Santa's Sleigh Day - Haiku

Santa's sleigh day, oh
Santa's really fun sleigh day
Around it all goes!

Katie Robinson (8)
Austin Friars St Monica's Junior School

Reindeer - Haiku

Reindeer with Santa
He has antlers and some hooves
He lives with Santa.

Sofia Feghali (7)
Austin Friars St Monica's Junior School

Haiku

The otter swims lots
To catch its slippery prey
Then it goes away.

William Martyn Ewart (8)
Austin Friars St Monica's Junior School

The Beaver - Haiku

A beaver can swim
They build dams with fallen trees
Beavers are quite cute.

Joseph Waterfield (7)
Austin Friars St Monica's Junior School

The Baiji - Haiku

The baiji can swim
Baiji swim underwater
Some baijis can jump.

Rafe Houston (7)
Austin Friars St Monica's Junior School

The Bear - Haiku

Bears can growl and stomp
They capture their prey and eat
They're sly and vicious.

Edward Anthony Mullock (8)
Austin Friars St Monica's Junior School

Hens And Cockerels - Haiku

A hen is a bird
A cockerel wakes you up
They peck at their food.

Samuel Wilson (7)
Austin Friars St Monica's Junior School

Haiku

The camel has humps
Camels are very grumpy
They are very slow.

Courtney Reynolds (7)
Austin Friars St Monica's Junior School

Dolphin - Haiku

The dolphin is blue
They jump and play in the sea
And catch fish to eat.

Isabella Mullock (8)
Austin Friars St Monica's Junior School

Fish - Haiku

My new goldfish swims
Around underwater, *glug*
What else do they do?

Ellie Graham (7)
Austin Friars St Monica's Junior School

My Cat - Haiku

My cat bites a lot
He eats salmon every day
And scratches most days!

Alyshia Gill (7)
Austin Friars St Monica's Junior School

Tiger - Haiku

Tigers have some stripes
The tiger jumps and kills its
Prey then eats it up.

Gregor Ian Gilchrist (7)
Austin Friars St Monica's Junior School

The Giraffe - Haiku

The giraffe has spots
It has a very long neck
And eats leaves above.

Bryony Temple (8)
Austin Friars St Monica's Junior School

The Little Dolphin - Haiku

Dolphins splash people
They are fancy and sparkly
All in one fish swim.

Eve White (8)
Austin Friars St Monica's Junior School

The Kitten - Haiku

I'm getting a cat
And it is for my birthday
It will live at Gran's!

Eve Elise Jamieson (7)
Austin Friars St Monica's Junior School

Baiji - Haiku

The baiji can swim
Watch them jumping in mid-air
See them glance at you.

Olivia Jane Fisher (7)
Austin Friars St Monica's Junior School

Anger

A nger is bright, hot, red like a firework in the sky
N ight-time the volcano erupts
G rass bends when strong wind blows
E verywhere is the smell of burnt toast and the sound of dogs barking
R ivers raging angrily.

Harrington Moore (9)
Austin Friars St Monica's Junior School

Pain

Pain is the popping, exploding pop
Grey are the dark shadows that come over and give pain
Pain is the burning hot curries that set your stomach on fire
The vicious cat's claws digging in my arm like a boat sinking in the sea
A volcano exploding, giving the sound of pain in my ears.

Gayathri Nair (8)
Austin Friars St Monica's Junior School

The Elephant - Haiku

Hey, don't you squirt me
Elephant, oh elephant
You are so pesky!

Jodi Wilkinson (7)
Austin Friars St Monica's Junior School

The Little Dolphin - Haiku

The dolphin is cute
Dolphins blend in with the sea
See them kiss at you.

Jessie Brown (7)
Austin Friars St Monica's Junior School

Excitement

Excitement is sapphire-blue just like the sky with doves flying, looking
for food
Hearing the doves cooing
It tastes like the sea salt fresh from the sea
The smell of fresh air on top of a high mountain
The warmth of the sun on your skin
It reminds me of me and my family playing in the garden together.

Jane Irving (8)
Austin Friars St Monica's Junior School

Anger

Anger is steamy-black
The sound of nails scratching a blackboard
It's like a venomous snake approaching slowly, waiting to kill
It looks like a volcano erupting
It feels like burnt dragon scales
Anger dwells in the depths of Hell.

John Colwell (9)
Austin Friars St Monica's Junior School

Happiness

Happiness is the great golden sun glistening like a diamond
The most tastiest of sweet sugar
It smells cleaner than the most beautiful flowers
It has the most fruitful sound of the purest of music
It is like bathing in the most gleeful joy
And the pleasure of seeing a dear old friend again.

Ailsa Duncan (8)
Austin Friars St Monica's Junior School

Stress

Stress, the dripping of fear
Venom falling from a tap
The sour taste of dry volcano rock
Medusa's stare, turn to stone
A knife digging into you
As strong as war pressing against you
The power of a centaur.

Bruce Long (9)
Austin Friars St Monica's Junior School

The Lion - Haiku

The lion is sly
Against his prey he catches
All in one it goes.

Sarah Margaret Long (8)
Austin Friars St Monica's Junior School

Fear

Fear is blood dripping from a vampire's fangs
A dark hole with monsters creeping out
Night-time and dark souls blazing fire
Ghosts floating around waiting for you
Fear is a dead person living
A haunted house with skeletons creeping.

Thomas Harrison (9)
Austin Friars St Monica's Junior School

Anger

As red as the reddest volcanoes
As black as a spider making a web on a shiny new wall
The loud sound of elephants marching on the road
Blood as hot as the hottest curry in India
It's as big as fire burning in the sun
Rough as jagged stones at the seaside.
Anger!

Isabel Leitch (9)
Austin Friars St Monica's Junior School

Anger

Anger is like the reddest hottest fire burning through a building
Scorching anything in its way
It smells like rotten bananas
It feels like the end of a razor-sharp knife
The taste of a sour lemon.

Joseph Logue (9)
Austin Friars St Monica's Junior School

Crazy

C razy is great fun
R evenge is part of the craziness
A nd some people like to be crazy
Z igzags are crazy
Y ellow is the colour of the Simpsons, the craziest of all.

Adrian Anderson (8)
Austin Friars St Monica's Junior School

Anger

Anger, the dark red and black
Crash, bang, two planets colliding
Fire on my tongue, *bang, bang!*
The reek from a cigarette
My brain will blow up
Little bugs crawling on my eye
A volcano erupting
Anger!

William Ferdinand (9)
Austin Friars St Monica's Junior School

Stress

Stress is like a great blazing fire
As loud as thunder
As quick as lightning
The taste of mouldy potatoes
As dark as darkest night
The smell of ash all around
As old as the oldest skeleton.

Rory Sutton (9)
Austin Friars St Monica's Junior School

Fear

F ear is as purple as squid's ink,
E villy squeezed into the world.
A pples going rotten, maggots crawling,
R ank swamps with creatures crawling.

Daniel Lumb (9)
Austin Friars St Monica's Junior School

Angry

A nger is really, really bad
N itrogen catches fire
G reat volcanoes erupt
R aging fury inside
Y ou need to let it out.

Harry Blowing (9)
Austin Friars St Monica's Junior School

Crazy

C razy is like flashing colours
R age is silliness in the air
A rcades full with people going crazy
Z ig and zag, people running about
Y o-yos going up and down.

Rupert Rosindell (9)
Austin Friars St Monica's Junior School

Crazy

C razy is fireworks round and round
R age of silliness in the air
A nd zebra crossings, black and white
Z ombies will have you hypnotised
Y ou're crazy, crazy, *crazy!*

Molly Pattinson (8)
Austin Friars St Monica's Junior School

Anger!

Oh no it's back, it's hotter than the sun
It's a volcano exploding every second
It's taller than Mount Everest
It tastes like ashes and it makes you go bad into the death-trap
Everything you touch turns into fire
It's black, black smoke
I wouldn't go near it or it might come out.

Niccolo Vetta (9)
Austin Friars St Monica's Junior School

Excitement

Excitement is popping in your head, waiting to burst out
Purple and orange are its colours
Mintoes and Coke bursting out in fountains
Popcorn popping, fireworks swirling
Twirling round like Catherine wheels
Sparkling, fizzing and popping.

Kathryn Orr (9)
Austin Friars St Monica's Junior School

Excitement

Oh excitement
I love it when it fizzes inside me
Just like I've eaten a bowl of sugar
And then you start running around like a mad baboon
Like Diet Coke and Mintoes together.

Arron Francis (9)
Austin Friars St Monica's Junior School

Happiness

Happiness makes me do good things
I think that happiness is yellow because it is bright and shiny
I like it very much.

Happiness is so good
It doesn't make me cry or shout
If I was a billionaire, tears of happiness I do try.

I will always try to do my best
Happiness is fun, it makes me laugh
If you play with happiness, I will play with you.

If you think happiness is bad
You're wrong, it's great
If you think of happiness when you sleep
You will dream and dream and dream.

I think you should play with happiness
Because you learn new things you never learnt before
If you play with happiness I will play too.

Joy Brouillard (10)
Austin Friars St Monica's Junior School

Anger

Anger is roaring in your brain
Feeling like you would explode
It tastes squishy and bitter
Smells like lava and fire
I wish it would stop
I wish! I wish!

Ho Yu Liu (9)
Austin Friars St Monica's Junior School

Happy

Happy feels
Exploding and blasting into space
Tastes like chocolate treats, tinsel and friends.

Happy is
Holidays and family, presents and fun
Birthdays, good times, games and music.

Spread happiness to the world!

Happy feels like
A smile, a handshake
A present, a cuddle.

Being nice to people
Surprises, treats
Happy feels like a warm smile.

Chay Tuuer-Richards (10)
Austin Friars St Monica's Junior School

That Awful Year

My fear is like a butterfly ready to go
To spread its wings and run.

The running, hitting, shouting of all that fear
David swearing and trying to scare me.

Every day especially on Friday,
Friday, the red blood dripping down and tears

How I wish, I wish I had a crown
Then I could order him around
So many people scared
One year felt like two, felt like three.

Cameron Gilchrist (9)
Austin Friars St Monica's Junior School

Happy Times

The lovely fun holidays away
A bright yellow sun shining in the sky
It tastes like eating something nice like cake
It feels like running your hand down a pony's back.

The exciting birthdays with friends
With a bright orange flame on a candle
It tastes like your mouth is burning with excitement.

Easter, a time to have chocolate eggs
There is no need for mums to bake
It tastes like delicious milk chocolate
It feels like the secret bunny's fur.

Christmas is a time to have Christmas trees
With all different colours like red
It tastes like bangs from Christmas crackers
It feels like a ribbon off a present.

Tara Houston (9)
Austin Friars St Monica's Junior School

Some Fears Of The World

Fear is like a bullet ready to hit, like a dark alley
Fear is like cutting yourself but you don't know what did it
Like a dark forest you are walking in, maybe a wolf waiting to attack.

Fear is like the darkest of oceans
Like the ocean, maybe a great white shark waiting to attack
Fear is like swimming in the ocean maybe something lurking
                                         behind you
Like darkness of an ocean, something waiting, waiting to attack.

Fear is like a dark forest of creatures lurking round you
Like a dark forest, a tiger waiting to kill you
Fear is like a dark forest at night and then they will jump on you
Like a dark forest you are walking in.

Blair Douglas (10)
Austin Friars St Monica's Junior School

Tiger's Rage

Anger feels like a tiger ripping through my fist
Anger smells like smoke from a fire
Anger tastes like a rotten apple
Anger looks like a cloud of black thunder.

Anger feels like sandpaper across your face
Anger smells like a pig's dinner
Anger tastes like burnt toast
Anger looks like a volcano exploding over my house.

Anger feels like getting hit by an express train
Anger smells like raw meat
Anger tastes like dirt from the ground
Anger looks like a hurricane ripping up your house.

Anger feels like a sword going through my heart
Anger smells like a dead corpse
Anger tastes like tears of sorrow
Anger looks like a tsunami washing away the happiness.

Robbie Ewart (9)
Austin Friars St Monica's Junior School

The Untrustworthy Penguin

I once had a penguin called Ozey
He was terribly bossy
One day he built an igloo
Of the whereabouts I never knew
So I set off to find it one day
I went to the North Pole
Turns out that's where it lay!

Gemma Stacey (11)
Austin Friars St Monica's Junior School

Happiness

It tastes like chocolate melting
It smells like you've achieved something
It looks like a rainbow
It feels like silk.

It might be the colour of yellow
It's as soft as a pillow
It's as sweet as sugar
It's colourful too.

Happiness is like good thoughts
Just like strawberries and cream
Happiness makes me cheerful
It makes me feel like I am on holiday.

Happiness is what matters to me
Happiness is as rough as nothing
Happiness is brilliant
Happiness is what makes the world glimmer.

Charlie Graham (9)
Austin Friars St Monica's Junior School

Suttie The Cat

Suttie the cat is black and white
And in the dark her eyes glow bright.

She catches all the small white mice
That do indeed taste very nice.

But now she is getting very old
And spends her last days out in the cold.

Logan Davidson (10)
Austin Friars St Monica's Junior School

Love

Love makes me think of family
Love makes me think of friends
Love makes me think of animals
Love makes me think most of all of peace.

Love is where the heart is
Love tastes like strawberries
Love makes me think of red wine
Love is very warm.

It's perfect and good
It's like a flower opening
It's much more special than gold
It's like family, friends . . . and everything together.

Most of love you'll get at Christmas
You will find lots of it in families
It's in your own life
You can learn very much from it.

And the good thing about it is
That you don't have to pay
You can give it to everybody
Freely, thankfully, happily.

Kimberly Bennett (10)
Austin Friars St Monica's Junior School

The Kangaroo

Look at him bounce side to side
Wouldn't it be a wonderful ride?

If you get too close to his baby
He will go absolutely crazy.

His fur is as soft as a pillow
Isn't he one jolly fellow?

I love the kangaroo
And if you respect him
He'll love you too.

Jack Freshwater (11)
Austin Friars St Monica's Junior School

Sadness

Sadness tastes like dry bread
No jam or butter
The salty sea at the beach on a winter's day
Or a bad banana.

The feel of cold sweat running down my face
A snail crawling across my hand
My friend leaving the room
You feel like you are sinking below the ground.

Sadness smells like a bitter lemon
Wet paper
An old potato
Or a rotten egg.

Sadness is a dark room
My heart sinking down to my toes
The door locking behind me
Or the world turning grey in front of my eyes.

Hannah McMillan (10)
Austin Friars St Monica's Junior School

The Monkey

The monkey swings from tree to tree
High and low, above the sea
And when he comes out to play
All the birds they fly away.

He has short brown fur
When he runs he is a blur
His eyes are green
And they're always seen!

At the end of the day, he sits down in bed
He thinks of the things he'd rather do instead
When the next day comes
He jumps up, ready to play!

Alice Tod (11)
Austin Friars St Monica's Junior School

Anger

Anger is yellow, orange and red
Anger tastes like lava set on fire
Anger feels like you are going to explode
Anger is set off by someone screaming at me.

Anger smells like fire burning wood
The texture of anger is like sharp spikes
Anger looks like a volcano exploding
Anger is like a monster set on fire.

Anger is a snake about to bite
Anger is a savage cat about to jump
Anger is a volcano about to erupt
Anger is a fire burning a forest down.

Anger is a wave knocking a wall down
Anger is a tornado blowing a tower down
Anger is an earthquake knocking a bridge over
Anger is lava covering a desert island.

Edwin Wilson (9)
Austin Friars St Monica's Junior School

The Panda

Silently, we draw near
Its great presence freezing us
In time
King-like, emperor
We watch in astonishment
Enthroned in silence
A majestic paw bestowing
Honour on the chosen
Stem
Snap!
One more tasty morsel
For the master
Of all he surveys
The panda.

William Stonebridge (11)
Austin Friars St Monica's Junior School

The Bengal Tiger

The tiger is like a hunter
It hides in its glowing golden fur
It lies in the forest
It pushes out its tough chest.

In the dark it eats
It eats any meats
The murderer lies in its lair
With the deer's blood in its hair.

It awakes
It eats what it takes
He is a giant
Who's defiant!

Chloe Isla Thomson (10)
Austin Friars St Monica's Junior School

What Is Pink?

(Based on 'What is Pink' by Christina Rossetti)

What is pink?
A rose is pink
Glittering, shining, makes you blink.

What is blue?
A river is blue
Wishing, washing, makes you need the loo.

What is gold?
A sunset is gold
It's so bright it makes you bold.

What is green?
The grass is green
With glittering flowers in-between.

What is white?
Jack Frost is white
With all of his might.

Laura Maden (9)
Beetham CE Primary School

What Is Pink?

(Based on 'What is Pink?' by Christine Rossetti)

What is blue?
The sky is blue, nice and blue.
What is yellow?
A banana is yellow, saying hello.
What is gold?
A ring is gold, rusty and old.
What is red?
A bed is red walking on my head.
What is black?
Night is black like Santa's sack.
What is grey?
A desk is grey talking to itself.
What is silver?
A star is silver, bright and light.
What is pink?
A flower is pink in a vase by my sink.

Ryan Williamson (8)
Beetham CE Primary School

What Is Pink?

(Based on 'What is Pink?' by Christina Rossetti)

What is pink?
A rose is pink.
What is gold?
A ring is gold.
What is red?
Silk is red
What is blue?
A river is blue.
What is yellow?
A banana is yellow.

Sam Maden (7)
Beetham CE Primary School

What Is Pink?

(Based on 'What is Pink' by Christina Rossetti)

What is blue?
Water is blue
I flush it down the loo.

What is pink?
A lipstick is pink
It is so bright it will make you blink.

What is black?
Coal is black
Put it in your sack.

What is red?
A bed is red
It is where I rest my head.

What is gold?
A ring is gold
What I love to hold.

What is grey?
The sky is grey
It makes me sad every day.

What is yellow?
A pillow is yellow
At night-time I say hello.

Annalise Harry (9)
Beetham CE Primary School

What Is Gold?

(Based on 'What is Pink?' by Christina Rossetti)

What is gold?
A ring is gold
I am told.

What is black?
A duck is black
It says quack.

What is red?
A poppy is red
In the flowerbed.

What is green?
Leaves are green
Little leaves of a bean.

What is blue?
Water is blue
A stream running beside you
With a fish passing through.

What is turquoise
A box is turquoise
That is cuboid.

Ella Handy (8)
Beetham CE Primary School

Love

Love is red like a big love heart
Love sounds like a girl singing
Love tastes like a lovely rice pudding
Love smells like roses
Love looks like a beautiful girl
Love feels like trying
Love reminds me of my mum and dad.

Dylan Beaty (8)
Belle Vue Junior School

Love

Love is red like a lollipop
Love sounds like my little brother laughing
Love tastes like a chocolate cookie
Love smells like a chocolate brownie
Love looks like my little brother
Love feels like a hug
Love reminds me of my family.

Callum Currie (8)
Belle Vue Junior School

Love

Love is red like a big love heart
Love sounds like a bird singing
Love tastes like chocolate
Love smells like a red rose
Love looks like a butterfly
Love feels like my sister Lily
Love reminds me of Mum and Dad.

Abigail Box (8)
Belle Vue Junior School

Laughter

Laughter is blue like a big tear
Laughter tastes like blueberries
Laughter smells like water
Laughter feels like wriggling
Laughter reminds me of love.

Kevan Coady (7)
Belle Vue Junior School

Love

Love is red like a red bird
Love sounds like music
Love tastes like chocolate
Love smells like sweets
Love looks like my mam and dad
Love feels like a singing bird
Love reminds me of my grandma's chocolate cake.

Ellis Dickinson (7)
Belle Vue Junior School

Love

Love is red like a sunflower
Love sounds like a flower with bees on
Love tastes like fudge
Love smells like cookies
Love looks like a puppy
Love feels like a firework
Love reminds me of my two cats, Buttons and Binky.

Robert Dalgliesh (7)
Belle Vue Junior School

Love

Love is red like a love heart
Love tastes like chocolate
Love smells sweet
Love looks like birds
Love feels like a pizza
Love reminds me of my mum and dad.

Joe Dawson (8)
Belle Vue Junior School

Love

Love is red like our beautiful heart
Love sounds like a bright red robin
Love tastes like chocolate cake
Love smells like spaghetti Bolognese
Love looks like a kiss
Love feels gorgeous
Love reminds me of every day when my mam gives me a kiss.

Jamie Graham (7)
Belle Vue Junior School

Laughter

Laughter is cold like bubbles
Laughter sounds like toys
Laughter tastes like pizza
Laughter smells like chocolate
Laughter looks like clowns
Laughter feels like my bed
Laughter reminds me of my television.

Bailey Gregan (7)
Belle Vue Junior School

Love

Love is like a spark
Love sounds like a flower
Love tastes like a sweet
Love smells like a steak
Love looks like a flower
Love feels like a hug
Love reminds me of my guinea pig.

Matthew Elliott (7)
Belle Vue Junior School

Love

Love is red like the colour of a heart
Love sounds like a dog barking
Love tastes like chocolate
Love smells like cakes
Love looks like a little flower
Love feels like a teddy bear
Love reminds me of my mum and dad.

Sarah Irving (8)
Belle Vue Junior School

Love

Love is pink like a flower
Love sounds like music
Love tastes like tomatoes
Love smells like kiwi fruit
Love looks like swimming
Love feels like softness
Love reminds me of Nana Audrey.

Megan Halliburton (7)
Belle Vue Junior School

Love

Love is red like a rose
Love sounds like a bird
Love tastes like chocolate
Love smells like roses
Love looks like my dog
Love feels like pizza
Love reminds me of my nana.

Richard Hope (8)
Belle Vue Junior School

Love

Love is red like a love heart
Love sounds like a beating heart
Love tastes like a Cyberman
Love smells like Rose Tyler
Love looks like a Dalek
Love feels like jelly
Love reminds me of my gran and Picnic my rabbit.

Ellie Johnson (7)
Belle Vue Junior School

Love

Love is like a love heart
Love sounds like roses
Love tastes like chocolate
Love smells like purple violets
Love looks like someone really happy
Love feels like dandelions
Love reminds me of my mam and dad.

Adam Lofthouse (7)
Belle Vue Junior School

Love

Love is like a big red heart
Love sounds like my favourite song
Love tastes like pizza
Love feels like my mum and dad
Love reminds me of my dog.

Lewis Jamieson (8)
Belle Vue Junior School

Love

Love is deep red like the colour of a heart
Love sounds like my brother being smart
Love tastes like sweet red apples
Love smells like lavender and vanilla
Love looks like my best ever friend
Love feels like a fluffy little kitten
Love reminds me of my old dog, Polly.

Rosie Steele (8)
Belle Vue Junior School

Love

Love is pink like roses
Love sounds like peace
Love tastes like chocolate
Love smells like bacon
Love looks like a star
Love feels like soft cushions
Love reminds me of my nanny.

Jonathan Peacock (7)
Belle Vue Junior School

Love

Love is red like a heart
Love sounds like music
Love tastes like pizza
Love smells like a red rose
Love looks like beauty
Love feels like a soft cushion.

Patrick Moore (8)
Belle Vue Junior School

Love

Love is red like a big red love heart
Love sounds like an apple crunching
Love tastes like chocolate
Love smells like grass
Love looks like my bed
Love feels like a teddy bear
Love reminds me of my mum and dad.

Karl Gibson (8)
Belle Vue Junior School

Love

Love is red like a heart
Love sounds like music playing
Love tastes like toffee
Love smells like flowers
Love looks like an apple
Love feels like a teddy
Love reminds me of my family.

Amber Surtees (8)
Belle Vue Junior School

Love

Love is a red heart
Love sounds like a song
Love smells like a red rose
Love tastes like sweets
Love looks like my mum and dad.

Brooke Stephenson (7)
Belle Vue Junior School

Love

Love is colourful like a rainbow
Love sounds like birds singing
Love tastes like a sweet apple
Love smells like flowers
Love looks like hearts
Love feels like soft flowers
Love reminds me of fruit.

Ben Walker (8)
Belle Vue Junior School

Love

Love is red like violets
Love looks like a stream
Love tastes like blossom
Love feels like kindness
Love smells like hearts
Love reminds me of my mam.

Lewis Young (8)
Belle Vue Junior School

Space

S hooting in the sea-blue sky
P assing all the amazing planets
A s the astronauts shake in their seats
C omets slowly passing by
E arth fades away in the distance.

Reece McLaughlin (10)
Belle Vue Junior School

Opposites

As loud as a lion roaring as fierce as he can
As quiet as a little brown mouse looking for orange cheese.

As fast as a speeding red car racing on a road
As slow as a tortoise travelling on a bumpy road.

As bright as a blazing hot sun on a summer's day
As dark as a black box buried under the ground full of old books.

As hard as a boulder thrown into your garden
As soft as a furry cushion sitting on your bed.

As thin as a pencil sitting on your desk ready for writing
As fat as a Sumo fighting his friends and throwing him to the ground.

Jamie Ruddick (7)
Belle Vue Junior School

Opposites

As hot as the blazing hot fire keeping us warm in the cold dark house
As cold as an ice-cold winter's day when you can see your own breath.

As fast as a cheetah hunting for his prey on a warm hot day
As slow as a snail leaving its trail along the ground.

As light as the big sun shining in the sky
As dark as the cold moon at night, high in the sky.

Ben Lancaster (7)
Belle Vue Junior School

Opposites

As soft as a sponge when it has soaked up all the water
As hard as a rock made of granite which I cannot smash.

As black as the midnight sky at night when everyone is asleep
As white as a polar bear away in Antarctica blending in with the snow.

As powerful as a knight with his shiny armour on
As weak as an ant when it is scuttling along the grass.

As fat as an elephant as it chews on its food
As thin as a twig swinging on a branch in the wind.

As fast as a zebra charging away from the lions
As slow as a tortoise trampling along the desert.

Jasmine Heaton (7)
Belle Vue Junior School

Opposites

As fast as a hare running a mile away
As slow as a turtle trampling along a sandy beach.

As soft as a ginormous elephant in the jungle
As thin as a snake slithering along to its prey.

As soft as a pillow helping me to sleep
As hard as a rock falling down a cliff.

As cold as the frozen water on the pond
As hot as the blazing sun.

Nathan Halliburton (8)
Belle Vue Junior School

Opposites

As light as a scuttling mouse in a mouse hole
As heavy as the giant Eiffel Tower in France.

As fast as a rocket to the moon
As slow as a baby snail trying to catch its mother in the grass.

As shiny as the tin foil on your sandwiches in a packed lunch
As dull as a piece of dark blue card sitting in a drawer, unused.

As big as the Statue of Liberty on the sea in New York
As small as a fat, hairy, rat living in an old house.

As hot as the blazing, scorching, hot sun
As cold as an Antarctic igloo with people inside wearing furry coats.

Jordan Armstrong (8)
Belle Vue Junior School

Opposites

As dark as a dungeon deep down in a castle
As light as a light shining across the street.

As fast as a hare shooting across the stone path
As slow as a slithery snake leaving a slimy trail.

As hot as a fire coming towards me
As cold as an ice cream dribbling on my hands.

Katie McGarr (7)
Belle Vue Junior School

Opposites

As powerful as a speeding cheetah hoping to catch his prey
As weak as a newborn chick trying to balance and catch up
                                    with its quicker mother.

As hot as the gleaming hot sun keeping us warm on a sunny
                                    summer's day
As cold as ice melting in the hands from the pond.

As loud as a lion roaring at its wife
As quiet as a squeaky mouse in her cosy home.

As dry as an elephant's skin as you feel its lumpy, bumpy back
As wet as a snake's scaly slimy body.

Catherine Brown (7)
Belle Vue Junior School

Opposites

As big as the Eiffel Tower swaying in the wind, a little bit anyway
As small as a little piece of sugar which my mum is about to eat.

As heavy as a big, fat elephant rolling in the mud
As light as a feather floating in the wind.

As slow as a very small snail going down the massive wall
As fast as a laughing hyena as he chases his prey to feed his children.

As old as my uncle who is 95 tiptoeing around his room
As new as brand new Lacoste trainers which I wear.

Robbie Bell (7)
Belle Vue Junior School

Opposites

As loud as a band playing a song
As quiet as a mouse living in a crack in a wall.

As big as an aircraft carrier waiting for a signal
As small as an atom in a table.

As dry as a bomb when it is about to explode
As wet as a beached whale, big and old.

As heavy as a monster truck steaming on a track
As light as a baby monkey in the forest swinging round the trees.

As soft as a teddy in my bed
As hard as steel on a machine.

Mark Palmer (8)
Belle Vue Junior School

Opposites

As fast as a cheetah catching its prey
As slow as a tortoise staggering along the garden path.

As fat as a hippo running through the forest
As thin as my eyelashes curled around my eyelids.

As hot as the scorching sun shining in the desert
As cold as the Antarctic where everything's white.

Austin McVittie (7)
Belle Vue Junior School

Opposites

As hot as the blazing stars in the giant galaxy
As cold as a freezing ice cream in a chilly freezer.

As big as the huge great Sphinx in the amazing Egyptian desert
As small as a baby ant hiking up a mountain.

As long as a winding snake slithering through the truly beautiful
long grass
As short as a newborn baby just out of its mum
As dark as Pluto on a bitter, raw, frosty, winter's day.

Samuel Simpson (8)
Belle Vue Junior School

Opposites

As hot as a blazing bonfire on November the 5th
As cold as the winter's snow which I can use to build a snowman.

As fast as a cheetah hunting for its prey in the jungle
As slow as a snail trying to move along on a stony path.

As powerful as the blazing sun
As weak as a sheet of paper that's been ripped and put in the bin.

As dark as a cave cut into rock
As light as the staggering moonlit sky at night full of silver stars.

Harry Caven (8)
Belle Vue Junior School

Opposites

As fast as a spotty cheetah racing for his dinner
As slow as an old tortoise trampling on the green grass.

As thin as a stick insect sliding on the leaves
As fat as an elephant standing and blowing his trunk really loudly.

As hard as a book on my school shelf
As soft as a bird's feather floating from the sky.

As powerful as a fox biting through a chicken
As weak as a baby giraffe wobbling on his long thin legs.

As hot as the sun melting my ice cream
As cold as a snowflake falling on my nose.

Brodie Stephenson (7)
Belle Vue Junior School

Opposites

As hot as a burning sauna just like a red-hot summer's day
As cold as the freezing cold Ice Age when animals such as
mammoths existed.

As fat as I feel when I've eaten too much of Mum's roast chicken
As thin as a skinny ant on patrol in a garden.

As dark as when it's lights off and something scary happens
As light as a sycamore helicopter falling to the ground.

Oliver Morley (8)
Belle Vue Junior School

Opposites

As hot as the hot blazing sun on a summer's day
As cold as the winter's ice as I touch it with my fingers.

As fast as an aeroplane speeding through the clouds
As slow as a turtle trampling along a beach.

As fat as a huge greedy elephant splashing around in a mud bath
As thin as me breathing in so I get thinner and thinner.

As smooth as a curved piece of granite
As hard as some pebbles sticking out of a wall.

As tall as the very high Eiffel Tower
As small as a furry mouse trying to hide from a scary cat.

Harrison Edgar (8)
Belle Vue Junior School

Opposites

As dark as a spooky dark night as I lie awake in bed
As light as a lamp shining beside you when you do your homework.

As fast as a zooming spotty cheetah running to get a piece of chicken
As slow as a tortoise tottering along a muddy path.

As hot as a burning, bright red fire burning a piece of wood
As cold as the deep dark ocean.

As heavy as a dark leather sofa when it's cosy
As light as a piece of paper lying on the floor.

Bethany Rutherford (8)
Belle Vue Junior School

Opposites

As fast as the train on the roller coaster as it spins round
As slow as a baby going to sleep holding his cute little teddy bear.

As hot as a blazing hot fire on Bonfire Night
As cold as winter's snow when I touch it with my hard hands.

As hard as rock as I pick it up with my tiny hands
As soft as a woolly jumper as I feel it when I put it on.

As dark as a cupboard as I walk through the door and get locked in
As light as the sun shining in my eyes and dazzling me.

Megan Abba (8)
Belle Vue Junior School

Opposites

As slow as a tortoise on our green grass
As fast as a cheetah catching its prey.

As hot as some lava surrounding the volcano
As cold as some ice down your back.

As small as a little pencil that's done lots of writing
As big as a big fat snake slithering through the long grass.

As soft as a comfy cushion to lay your head on
As hard as a big rock falling down a cliff.

Rebecca Connor (7)
Belle Vue Junior School

Opposites

As big as the massive Empire State Building in America
As small as a tiny ant looking for some food.

As hot as the blazing sun shining down from the sky
As cold as the frosty snow covering the car.

As fat as an elephant as it tries to run
As thin as a mouse's tail as a cat grabs it!

Lewis Dock (7)
Belle Vue Junior School

Opposites

As fast as a spotty cheetah running for his prey
As slow as a prickly hedgehog trampling on the long green grass.

As tall as a giraffe eating his meal from the high tree branches
As small as an ant running to his underground house.

As soft as a soft comfy cushion under my head
As hard as a rock sitting on some green grass.

As large as an elephant blowing his trunk as lively as he can
As tiny as a butterfly fluttering in the bright blue sky.

Sophie Todd (8)
Belle Vue Junior School

Opposites

As fast as a red blazing Ferrari car
As slow as a tiny little ant tramping through the grass.

As hot as the sun on a gleaming summer's day
As cold as an ice lolly melting in my hands.

As loud as a lion roaring in its cage
As quiet as an ant crawling on the stone path.

Leah Osgood (7)
Belle Vue Junior School

Guilt

I live deep down in the pounding of the black side of your heart
I only come out if you regret something
My colour is red - stirred with a touch of blue
I was born when you were
Can you guess who I am?
I am guilt!

James Hadden (10)
Belle Vue Junior School

Space Adventure!

S oaring into the pitch-black sky
P reparing to shout, 'Goodbye.'
A dmiring all the magnificent planets
C ooling down with a drink
E ventually getting to the moon

A stonishing views down below
D aniel taking some photos
V ibration on my lovely chair
E very time I look outside I see a comet passing by
N ight, I say to my friends
T ucking into my comfy chair
U ranus is just out there
R eally I can't help but stare
E ventually I will get back home and talk on my telephone.

James Nixon (10)
Belle Vue Junior School

My Space Poem

Walking into the great big rocket
Feeling claustrophobic with my hands in my pocket
Counting down from 10, 9, 8
Standing next to my best mate
Whizzing through the starry sky
Oh my goodness, I can fly
Floating softly onto evil Mars
Trying to find our space cars
Standing on the rocks and bumps
As you can feel all the lumps
Now I know what it is like
I can't wait to tell my brother, Mike
Eventually I am back on Earth
Thinking what memories are worth.

Rebecca Heyworth (10)
Belle Vue Junior School

Space Invaders

S ee the engineers all around
P osing like ants on the ground
A stronauts in the rocket
C arrying something in their pocket
E nding up on a different planet

I magining a better place
N oticing he hadn't tied his lace
V anishing into deep, dark space
A dventuring to the different worlds
D odging asteroids like little pearls
E choing throughout the solar system
R acing past the stars
S oftly landing on the ground.

Liam Dawson (10)
Belle Vue Junior School

Space

S itting in the vibrating chair
P reparing for a long bumpy launch
A dmiring all the scenery
C ramped inside a little rocket
E ventually arriving at our destination
S illy sound coming into the surface
H umming into the distance
I nteresting looking at the stars
P raying to the Lord, please bring us home safe.

Mark Lofthouse (10)
Belle Vue Junior School

Space

Going up into space
Floating in the sky
Feeling scared, sick and dizzy
Loudly vibrating in my chair
Fastly flying into space
Shaking nervously I cannot bear to look
There it goes, *bang, bang!*
The rocket shaking loudly
Now I am feeling lost in the air.

Connor McLaughlin (10)
Belle Vue Junior School

In To Space We Go

Anxiously listening . . . 10, 9, 8 . . .
Trying to keep themselves straight
Not even caring about the sun
Saying bye-bye to their only son
Looking at all the stars
NASA's favourite planet is Mars
Doing their first mission
Which had always been their ambition.

Cameron Keal (10)
Belle Vue Junior School

Mars

Nervously waiting to set off to Mars
Soon we will be whizzing faster than cars
Suddenly the engine starts frantically roaring
5, 4, 3, 2, 1, then we were soaring
Getting higher and higher up in space
I've never seen such a beautiful place
Finally landing on an amazing sight
After the long and vibrating flight.

Chloe Little (10)
Belle Vue Junior School

Blast-Off!

B lasting off to the stunning moon
L oving family waving back
A stronauts flying into the starry sky
S itting in the vibrating rocket
T ightly holding onto a picture

O pening the door to the moon
F inally we get back to Earth
F lying down to my friends.

Megan Fisher (10)
Belle Vue Junior School

A Summer's Day!

A watery-blue turns into a silky white
It's morning on a quiet summer's day
As the sign post just stands there alone
The smell of fresh fish just been caught
Out on a fishing trip is ghastly
A passer-by stops to feed the excited ducks
As the church bell rings!

Sam Abba (10)
Belle Vue Junior School

Space

S peechlessly walking into the crowded rocket
P assing the controllers, are we ready to go?
A t 12 noon we're up on the moon
C limbing down the rocket ladder
E arth, our home, is down below.

Susanna Whiffen (9)
Belle Vue Junior School

Can You Guess?

I live in the swollen red lump deep in your throat
My favourite colour is a deep purple with a layer of light grey
I was born when living things became deceptive and untrustworthy
I have no friends because nobody can trust me
I feed on your spirit and weaken your soul
My name is Guilt.

Lewis Harkins (11)
Belle Vue Junior School

?

I live deep down in the black rotten part of your stomach
I love stealing things and making people cry
My favourite colour is a dark frosty orange
I have long, green, dirty hair which I brush with my warts
My favourite food is spicy slimy slugs
My name is Jealousy.

Charlotte Harty (11)
Belle Vue Junior School

Sandy Summer

A lovely sky-blue mixed with a sandy-yellow
It's early evening on a shiny summer's day
As the boats are slowly drifting into the water
You can smell the swift salty sea air
As a passing car pulls over and goes to the sandy shore
While the boat drifts away.

Owen Dowie (10)
Belle Vue Junior School

The Best Summer's Day

Silk-white splashed by a muddy brown
Midday on a bright summer's day as swooping birds make
the weather-vane spin
The smell of overpowered, dead fish arriving back on a small
shiny boat
A boy biking past, eating a mouth-watering bacon sandwich
With brown sauce slathered all over, topped off with olive-green lettuce
Drinking a can of Coke.

Joseph Coates (11)
Belle Vue Junior School

Who Am I?

I live in a red-hot flaming volcano that erupts on every bad move
My hobbies are making you burst open at 200 degrees
I am a flaming red with a blaze of orange
My favourite colours are death-red with demon-orange
I kill all animals as they make people happy
I've been around since Earth began
I love fire or a bomb blowing up
My name is *Anger.*

Robbie Morley (11)
Belle Vue Junior School

Feelings

I live deep down in the cruel lurking parts of your souls
My favourite colour is blood-red
My favourite food is dead skin peeling from your body
I don't have time for hobbies because I'm so busy spreading misery
My name is *Pain!*

Sophie Armstrong (11)
Belle Vue Junior School

A Crisp Summer Morning

An olive-green blends with a pale watery blue
It's early morning on a bright summer's day
The crisp country air fills the land
I notice the tide coming in and splashing against the sandy shore
The dark mysterious mountains creep up into the blazing sunrise
Meanwhile, the sparkling golden sun peeps out from behind the
fluffy clouds.

Anna Robbins (11)
Belle Vue Junior School

Peaceful Seaside

Clear-white clouds in a beautiful blue sky
It's an early summer's morning as the trees are swaying
in the cool breeze
The smell from the fishing boats fills the air
There is a runner passing by as the boat floats into the distance.

Jamie Blair (11)
Belle Vue Junior School

Revenge

I live in the rock hard crunching knuckle
I feel the blood splashing against the knuckle
I like making blood squirt
I like to eat purple steak
I grow deep down in the stirring bloody guts
My name is Revenge.

Daniel Veitch (10)
Belle Vue Junior School

Who Am I?

I live in the fiery pit of your heart
I am the darkest, inkiest black
But I'm also as red as your blood
I came into the world when all time was forgotten
My pet is the devil of Hell, he is called Fire Master
My favourite food is a double-decker portion of blood-red chilli spine
My name is Hatred!

Ellen Johnston (11)
Belle Vue Junior School

. . . H . . .

I live in the deepest gloomiest part of your soul in a mist of blood
I am a bold black mixed with a ripe red
My hobbies are to knock my brother Anger
I feast on your soul when nobody knows
I have been around since you were born
But will always be here for when anyone upsets you
My name is *Hatred!*

Samantha Graham (10)
Belle Vue Junior School

Seashore

A bushy green blends to a baby-blue
It's an early afternoon on a bright summer's day
I also noticed the wooden boats coming in
As the smell of the salty sea swishing in
Where the graceful birds pass across the salty sea
As a family are having a stroll along the seashore.

Becky Osgood (11)
Belle Vue Junior School

Our Solar System

Our solar system looks like a burst of colour in your life
Stars popping up in the night sky trying to get your attention
Twinkling on the wall, can't get to sleep.

Trying to walk to school as the sun catches my eye
Late for tea as the stars come passing by
But still a beautiful day, still as beautiful at night.

Earth sounds like a happy world full of happy and joyful people
To loads of sound coming out of the world, still as happy.

Still looking in the sky, not a peep out of any planet up high in the sky
Still admiring the space shuttles.

Poppy Cutherbertson (9)
Belle Vue Junior School

Who Am I?

I live in a black cave below the beating heart
Feasting on the leftovers of scraps of thick red blood
I am a dragon-shaped shadow glowing in luminous green
I have a brother more horrid than me
I hoped to be black
I can't tell . . . I am the light
My life began when the heart pounded 100mph of shock
It's hard being cruel and mean
My job is travelling to the brain
To cause nightmares and unhappy sights.
My name is Fear.

Lauren Montgomery (10)
Belle Vue Junior School

Space

S pectacular view through Mars, Uranus and Neptune despite them
all being different sizes and colours I think they are perfect
just like our mothers

P lanets are like a big balloon floating and floating around the sun
like the moon

A stronauts vrooming into space with gigantic happy smiles
on their faces

C omets making craters and asteroids too, they will hopefully
not hit you

E arth is amazing, we all know that. We all know that because
that is a fact.

Joseph Harrison (9)
Belle Vue Junior School

Late On A Spring Afternoon

An olive-green rising up into a pale water blue
It's a late afternoon on a cloudy spring day
And the brownish path bordered by grey stones
Fades onto the soft yellow sand
The smell of fresh grass just been cut fills the air around me
Someone else strolling along the powdery sand must smell it too
Another boat comes into view
It's surrounded by rainbow-coloured scaly fish!

Molly Giles (11)
Belle Vue Junior School

?

I live in the deepest darkest parts of your soul
My favourite colour is misty purple with a drop of gloomy grey
I was born the same decade when time began
My brother is Hate and my sister is Anger
My favourite food is dark red blood
I have an overweight pet bulldog called Guilt
My name is Jealousy!

Lauryn Jamieson (10)
Belle Vue Junior School

Space

S tars in our solar system you may never travel to
P lanets orbiting around our sun
A stronauts floating about in outer space
C raters on the moon as big as Planet Earth
E arth, our planet, the only one with known life on it.

Aaran Atkinson (9)
Belle Vue Junior School

My Space

S tars are shining bright, on the dark and nasty night
P lanets in the night sky are the planets passing by
A liens are on the moon is it like Neptune?
C omets in the midnight sky, zooming fast by and by
E arth is really small, but not the smallest planet of them all.

Jamie Bradley (9)
Belle Vue Junior School

Space

S tars in the dark sky always twinkling up high
P lanets are big, some are small, how many are smaller than me
 And how many are bigger than me?
A stronauts flying up high past the planets, saying goodbye
C raters bang in the air, how loud would it be there?
E arth is where we live and is so bright in the light sky.

Chelsea Cairns (9)
Belle Vue Junior School

Space

S pace shuttles explore space with people inside
P lanets come in all different sizes
A stronauts going to space and discovering many things
C raters are all over the moon
E arth is the only planet with people on it.

Liam Short (9)
Belle Vue Junior School

Space

S olar system floating around us in the sky
P lanets orbiting round the sun in an orbital path
A stronauts exploring space in satellites and space stations
C raters on the moon where Neil Armstrong went
E arth, the planet where we live and the third planet from the sun.

Mark Donnelly (9)
Belle Vue Junior School

The Snowman

Flying over the icy sea
Dashing through frosty air
Houses look so very small
Snow-capped trees down below
Snow landing on the roof
Frosty world down over there
Calm as the mountains pass
Gently landing on the snow
Now he is fast asleep
Running outside excitedly
Devastated that it's melted
Crying now his friend has gone!

Oliver Bellingham (9)
Belle Vue Junior School

Space

I look up from Earth and try to see
A wonderful sight is shining at me
The stars twinkle bright
Then the moon shines a bright light
When I gaze I see a few planets
And I see Mercury, Venus or Mars, is it?
Magically I thought I saw the Milky Way
So I had to turn away
Longing, something wasn't right
Something was missing, the other five sights.

Hannah-Mae Graham (9)
Belle Vue Junior School

The Snowman

Flying over the glittery big world
Looking at all of the snowy roofs
People staring up at them
Seeing lots of silver shine
Cold up in the snowy air
Feeling scared up in the air
Thinking, *it is quiet up here*
Very cold in the air
As the snowman was melting
Landed on the soft snow
Boy very amazed
So sad and devastated
As the snowman was gone.

Nicole Atkinson (9)
Belle Vue Junior School

The Space Race

I look up from our world to see
All the planets staring back at me
The moon is shining ever so bright
In the misty but lovely night
Space shuttles setting off in the midnight sky
Visiting Pluto the one that is so shy
The solar system is a big, big sight
Especially when the stars are shining like a light.

Chloe Notman (9)
Belle Vue Junior School

Solar System!

S pectacular, shining and gleaming stars in the planets
  of all the red planet Mars
P luto, Pluto how small could it be? Is it the smallest planet
  or is it just me?
A stronauts flying up so high, far and far away and it's like
  we're saying goodbye
C raters, craters, how horrendous could they be?
  The crashing and bashing is so annoying to me
E choes, echoes as long as fifty miles, so cold but so long,
  how fast could it be?

Emma Bradley (9)
Belle Vue Junior School

Space

S pectacular stars glittering in the sky
P lanets go around and around the sun
A stronauts bring a burst of colours
C raters, they're all over the moon and Mars
E very person on the Earth gazing up at the twinkling stars.

Sophie Earl (9)
Belle Vue Junior School

Space

S paceships travel all over space
P lanets spin around
A stronauts walk on the moon
C omets shoot around in space
E arth is known as the blue planet.

Syd Harty (9)
Belle Vue Junior School

Space! Space!

S tars shining up high in the dark night sky
P lanet Earth tiny and small, but still most beautiful of them all
A stronauts flying in big mighty space shuttles up, up high
C raters fighting their way through war, hitting enemies, *ouch* that hurt
E arth still spinning round and round, while the sun goes down
    to sleep.

Charlotte Norman (9)
Belle Vue Junior School

Space

S tars shine in the sky at night
P luto is the smallest and furthest away planet from the sun
A stronauts explore space
C omets shoot through sky and space
E arth has over a zillion people on the planet.

Joseph Robson (9)
Belle Vue Junior School

The Adventure

S ilver star sparkling from so far
P aradise orbiting our sky up so high
A ll the planets travelling round the sun
C ome, it looks so much fun
E very time I watch them I feel happy.

Shaun Lester (9)
Belle Vue Junior School

Stunning Space

Stunning space shuttles shooting through the star-filled sky
Fireballs flying faster than fast
Astronauts thinking what can they accomplish?
Moons surrounding Mercury and of course, Mars
Fabulous Saturn, how beautiful it is
Crashing craters have been lying there for millions of years
People from Earth spending precious time watching space scurry by.

Niall Sanderson (9)
Belle Vue Junior School

Space

S tars you see brightly twinkling at night that you will never travel to
P lanets floating round the sun, all nine of them
A stronauts going planet to planet, floating round high in the sky
C omets look so much fun
E very time I see the solar system I know what I want to do
    When I'm older - land on the moon!

Matthew Story (9)
Belle Vue Junior School

Recipe For A Summer Holiday

Take a stretch of green grassy fields and loveable animals
Add on a rainy Tuesday morning
Sprinkle with light wind and rain
Cover with crisps, sandwiches, juice and cake
And wrap in warm photographs
To look at on cold wintry nights.

Caitlin Thomson (8)
Belle Vue Junior School

Recipe For A Summer Holiday

Take a stretch of the salty sea
And a sandy and rocky beach
Add a towel and suncream
Sprinkle with sandhoppers and silverfish
Cover with sun through the clouds
And wrap in funny photographs
To look at on boring days.

Orla Giles (8)
Belle Vue Junior School

Recipe For A Summer Holiday

Take a stretch of a colourful, cold, salty sea
And a super sandy sandwich
Add a swimming suit, bucket and a super spade
Sprinkle with super slimy sand
Cover with dripping ice cream
And wrap in a wet treasure towel
To look at on a perfect picture.

Rebecca Graham (8)
Belle Vue Junior School

Recipe For A Summer Holiday

Take a field full of strawberries and baskets
And four people to pick
Add lots of bushes
Sprinkle with strawberry juice, cover with cream
Wrap in yummy photos
To look at on December days.

Anna Ostridge (8)
Belle Vue Junior School

Recipe For A Summer Holiday

Take a stretch on a marsh
And a small gutter full of water
Add some binoculars and wellies
Sprinkle with heavy rain
Cover with colourful soggy coats
And wrap in loads of pictures
To look at on super sunny days.

Caitlin Humes (8)
Belle Vue Junior School

Recipe For A Summer Holiday

Take a stretch of sandy sea
And a fishing spot
Add a wakeboard, motorboat
And some scuba-diving equipment
Sprinkle with dripping ice cream
Cover with some soft sand
And wrap in some terrific towels
To feel on cold winter nights.

Jacob Bie (8)
Belle Vue Junior School

The Darkness

S olar system plus
P lanets
A ll around the world
C omets are rocks
E arth hardly gets hit.

Sophie Parker (9)
Belle Vue Junior School

Recipe For A Summer Holiday!

Take a stretch of sailing on the sea
A sail and lots of ropes
Add a life-jacket and a picnic
Sprinkle with splashes of the sea
Cover with coats and wetsuits
And wrap in fine photos
To look at on a freezing cold day.

Beth Giles (8)
Belle Vue Junior School

Recipe For A Summer Holiday

Take a stretch of cool water
And a sizzling hot dog
Add a fairground
Sprinkle with a hot summer's day
Cover with warm towels
And wrap in cold covers
To look at on hot days.

Ethan Skowronek (8)
Belle Vue Junior School

Space

S is for our spectacular solar system
P is for our super-sized planets
A is for our amazing astronomy
C is for our comets zooming to Earth
E is for our exceptional astronauts
    Space!

Thomas Wilson (9)
Belle Vue Junior School

Recipe For A Summer Holiday

Take a stretch on a sandy beach
And let the waves touch your feet
Add sandy towels and buckets and spades
Sprinkle with deckchairs and ice cream
Cover with sandcastles
And wrap in a warm towel
To look at on a winter's day.

Lucy Jackson (8)
Belle Vue Junior School

Recipe For A Summer Holiday

Take a stretch of sandy beach
And hot dogs covered in sand
Add an umbrella
Sprinkle with creamy buns
And cover with suncream
And wrap in a towel
To look at on the beach.

Hollie Notman (8)
Belle Vue Junior School

Recipe For A Summer Holiday

Take a hot sunny day in Penrith
And a bad dark cloud
Add having food in a family restaurant
Sprinkle with a cold jacket
Cover with loads of people
And wrap in colourful photographs
To look at on hot Sundays.

Matthew Segal (8)
Belle Vue Junior School

Recipe For A Summer Holiday

Take a stretch of a boat ride
And a swan and a cygnet
Add a life-jacket, oars and clear water
Sprinkle with black fish, green weed
Cricket players and stones
Cover with blazing hot sunshine
And wrap in funny photographs
To look at on a dull day.

April Coward (8)
Belle Vue Junior School

Recipe For A Summer Holiday

Take a stretch of a sandy beach
And a piece of sea
Add a surfboard with big waves
Sprinkle with thunder and lightning
Cover with a wild gorilla
And wrap in ice cubes as big as mini vans
To look at on a horrible dull day.

Matthew Ogilvie (9)
Belle Vue Junior School

Recipe For A Summer Holiday

Take a stretch of sun and sky and a surfer on the sea.
Add a cold refreshing orange juice.
Sprinkle with a burst of sunshine.
Cover with a soft blanket and wrap up in photographs
To look at on some stormy night.

Jonathon Veitch (8)
Belle Vue Junior School

Recipe

Take a stretch of a hot summer's day
And a gentle breeze off the sea
Add a barbecue and a drink of Coke fresh from the fridge
Also camel rides and stalls
Sprinkle with lots of fun
Deckchairs and lilos with people on top
Cover with a thick layer of sun.

Holly Aitchison (9)
Belle Vue Junior School

The Day The Zoo Escaped

The monkeys sailing out sneakily
The spiders creeping out quickly
The tigers marching out proudly
The rabbits skipping out brightly
The rats running out happily
The cheetahs zipping out suddenly
But the snail stubbornly staying in his shell.

Katie Keal (8)
Belle Vue Junior School

Recipe For A Summer Holiday

Take a stretch of a sandy beach
And a calm sea
Add a surfboard and a swimming costume
Cover with thick slices of sun
And wrap in colourful photographs
To look at on dark days.

Abbie McLaughlin (9)
Belle Vue Junior School

The Sound Collector

(Based on 'The Sound Collector' by Roger McGough)

'A stranger called this morning
Dressed in black and grey
Put every sound into a bag
And carried them away'.

The snorting of the pig
The rumble of a belly
The ping of the microwave
The wobbling of the jelly.

The laughing of the children
The sound of a croaking toad
The woof of a dog
The sound of a car going down the road.

'A stranger called this morning
He didn't leave his name
Left us only silence
Life will never be the same'.

Georgia Palmer (9)
Belle Vue Juniior School, Carlisle

Magic Box

(Based on 'Magic Box' by Kit Wright)

I will put in my box . . .
A flying pink mermaid
Someone walking in the green sky
The sound of birds tweeting in the trees
The sweet smell of lemon cheesecake
The feel of soft white feathers coming from the sky
The taste of sizzling sausages with blue tomato sauce.

My box is made out of pink sparkly wood
I would like to go on an adventure in my box.

Beth Bannister (9)
Belle Vue Junior School

The Sound Collector

(Based on 'The Sound Collector' by Roger McGough)

'A stranger called this morning
Dressed in black and grey
Put every sound into a bag
And carried them away'.

The growling of a dog
The tweeting of a bird
The humming of the milkman
The singing I heard.

The squelch of a riverbank
The creak of a door
The squeak of a mouse
The rumble of the floor.

'A stranger called this morning
He didn't leave his name
Left us only silence
Life will never be the same'.

Emily Frith (8)
Belle Vue Junior School

The Magic Box

(Based on 'Magic Box' by Kit Wright)

I will put in my box . . .
A silver shiny statue with diamonds on it
Like the sound of a mermaid.

I will put in my box . . .
A blue sky and a black dark sky
With stars on it and a flying mermaid above it.

I will put in my box . . .
An ice cream with sprinkles and marshmallows.

I will build my box out of clouds and water.

Victoria Boaden (8)
Belle Vue Junior School

The Sound Collector

(Based on 'The Sound Collector' by Roger McGough)

'A stranger called this morning
Dressed in black and grey
Put every sound into a bag
And carried them away'.

The swishing of the tap
The creaking of the gate
The ticking of the clock
The burning of the cake.

The roaring of the fire
The swishing of the fish
The bubbling of the fizzy drink
The purring of the cat
The hissing of the snake.

'A stranger called this morning
He didn't leave his name
He left us only silence
Life will never be the same'.

Isabel Harkins (9)
Belle Vue Junior School

Doughnut

Beer drinker
TV watcher
Stubble wearer
Not a carer
Doughnut eater
Lazy sleeper
Yellow faced
Sofa placed
Who am I?
A:Homer Simpson.

Thomas Blythe (10)
Belle Vue Junior School

Who Am I?

Famous singer
Piano player
Song lover
Band bringer
Song writer
Microphone owner
Queen member
Fan attracter
Guess who?
A: Freddie Mercury.

Sean Campbell (10)
Belle Vue Junior School

My Teacher!

M oments of surprise
, R aising his voice

H e's the best
A nnoying other teachers
R eading this poem with a smile
V ery special to us
E xotic attitude
Y ep, he's cool.

Emily Wiggett (10)
Belle Vue Junior School

Night Monster

D eathly roar
R aging terror
A mazing sight
G ore eater
O ngoing hunter
N ight freaker.

Maegan Witherington (10)
Belle Vue Junior School

Killer Instincts

Law breaker
Fight maker
Peace hater
Problem creator
Car leaker
House breaker
Gun holder
Life moulder
Hood wearer
Gang member
Who am I?

James Lewis Litherland (11)
Belle Vue Junior School

Peaceful But Harmful

Worm eater
Human treater
Hook finder
Peace minder
Journey taker
Germ maker
What am I?

Chloe Kerr (10)
Belle Vue Junior School

Aaargh!

Scary serpent
Mystical for certain
Deadly glare
No hair
All scales
Can't eat whales
Scares spiders
A very good hider
What am I?
A: Basilisk.

Lucy Thompson (10)
Belle Vue Junior School

Whispering

I'm not a colour
Not even white

I'm everywhere
Always there

Always around you
Always moving too

Got no taste
Got some pace

Who am I?
A: Air.

Liam Farish (11)
Belle Vue Junior School

Mischief

Banana stealer
Mischief wealder
Animal finder
Not getting kinder
Not very kind
Very, very blind
A big tree climber
Not getting finer
Eats lots of bugs
Doesn't give hugs
What am I?
A: Monkey.

Jack Lennon (10)
Belle Vue Junior School

Gigantor

G iant neck
I nteresting body
R eally tall
A gile tongue
F or the trees
F orever the biggest
E nergetic if needed.

Luke Surtees (11)
Belle Vue Junior School

Chinese New Year Poem

He's not good friends with cat
The first is the year of the rat.

He didn't swim in his socks
The next is the year of the ox.

With stripes the colour of fire
The next is the year of the tiger.

Jumping through the air
The next is the year of the hare.

As big as a wagon
The next is the year of the dragon.

Swimming across the lake
The next is the year of the snake.

Thundering along, of course
The next is the year of the horse.

Landing in a heap
The next is the year of the sheep.

His legs all big and chunky
The next is the year of the monkey.

Racing against the clock
The next is the year of the cock.

Floating on a log
The next is the year of the dog.

Munching a fig
The last is the year of the pig.

Kung shi fa choi!
Happy Chinese New Year!

**Skye Wohl, Sam Bailey, Teddy Birkbeck, & Oona Roberts (3),
Elizabeth Joyce, Francis Peers, Amelie Marshall
& Jane Mieras (4), Danny Poland (6), & Raf Appleby**
Blue Gate Montessori School, Carlisle

If You Want To See An Osprey

(Inspired by 'Alligator' by Grace Nichols)

If you want to see an osprey
You must go to the shiny shore
At Bassenthwaite Lake.

I know an osprey
Who's living down there
He's a flying, he's a fast,
He's a soaring one to watch.

Yes, if you really want to see an osprey
You must go to the shiny shore
At Bassenthwaite Lake.

Go down softly and say
Osprey zoom
Osprey zoom
Osprey zooooooom!

And she'll come down to you
But don't forget to scream!

Emily Speck (9)
Braithwaite CE (VA) Primary School

If You Want To See A Tiger

(Inspired by 'Alligator' by Grace Nichols)

If you want to see a tiger
You must go down to the hot Indian forest.

I know a tiger that's living down there -
She's a stripy, she's a fierce
She's a meat-eating machine.

Go down silently and say
Tiger Fred, Tiger Fred
Tiger Frreeeed.

And she will come out from the bushes
But don't stick around and try
Not to scream but run for your life!

Natalie Field (8)
Braithwaite CE (VA) Primary School

If You Want To See A Tiger

(Inspired by 'Alligator' by Grace Nichols)

If you want to see a tiger
You must go down to the dark creepy forest.

I know a tiger who's living down there
He's lovely, soft, stripy and fluffy.
Yes, if you really want to see a tiger
You must be nice and friendly.

Go down quietly and softly say
Tiger baby
Tiger baby
Tiger babyyyyyyy
And he'll pop his head out
But you might get scared and run away.

Amy Oxley (9)
Braithwaite CE (VA) Primary School

The Man From Bristol

There once was a man from Bristol
Who found a shiny crystal
He went to the shop
To buy a mop
But got shot by a nine-inch pistol.

Timmy Price (9)
Braithwaite CE (VA) Primary School

If You Want To See A Tiger

(Inspired by 'Alligator' by Grace Nichols)

If you want to see a tiger
You must go to the big, deep, dark, rainforest
I know a tiger who's living down there.

He's a fierce, he's a sneaky, he's a stripy thing
Yes, if you really want to see a tiger
You must go to the big, deep, dark, rainforest.

Go down to the deep dark forest and say
Tiger, tiger, fierce tiger
Tiger, tiger, fierce tiger
Tiger, tiger, fierce tigerrrr . . .
And run for your life, because he will bite.

Alex Halsall (7)
Braithwaite CE (VA) Primary School

Tigers

(Inspired by 'Alligator' by Grace Nichols)

If you want to see a tiger
You must go to a jungle, he'll be there
I know a tiger who's living down there
He's big, he's wild and he kills.

Yes, if you really want to see him
You must be very silent and careful
And say, *tiger come catch me*
I wouldn't want to disturb him
So run for your life!

Robert Saxton (8)
Braithwaite CE (VA) Primary School

If You Want To See A Tiger

(Inspired by 'Alligator' by Grace Nichols)

If you want to see a tiger
You must go to the deep dark wood

I know a tiger who's living down there
He's a furry and cuddly
If you really want to see a tiger
You must go to a muddy slushy wood
Go down carefully and say
Tiger, tiger, tiger
And don't stay for long
Or he will get you for good!

Jasmine Stubbs (8)
Braithwaite CE (VA) Primary School

If You Want To See A Tiger

(Inspired by 'Alligator' by Grace Nichols)

If you want to see a tiger
You must go down to the swampy squelchy swamp
I know a tiger who's living down there
He's a fighter, he's a catcher
He's a furry old chaser.

Yes, if you really want to see a tiger
You must go down sneakily to the swampy squelchy swamp
And say, baby tiger, baby tiger, baby tiger
And she'll sneak out
But don't stick around, *climb up a tree!*

Bethany Mawdsley (8)
Braithwaite CE (VA) Primary School

If You Want To See A Tiger

(Inspired by 'Alligator' by Grace Nichols)

If you want to see a tiger
You must go down to the swampy, dark, muddy shore
I know a tiger who's living down there
He's fierce, furry, he's stripy, he's a sneaky tiger too.

Yes, if you really want to see a tiger
You must go down to the swampy, dark, muddy shore
Go down, very far down and say
Stripy, stripy, stripy tiger
And he'll come out of the grass
But remember he's *fierce!*

Esther Tonkin (8)
Braithwaite CE (VA) Primary School

The Senses

Wouldn't it be funny if you didn't have a nose?
You couldn't tell a dirty nappy from a red rose!

Wouldn't it be boring if you didn't have a tongue?
You couldn't taste anything, not even meat that's hung!

Wouldn't it be boring if you couldn't touch?
You couldn't feel anything, not very much!

Wouldn't it be quiet if you didn't have ears?
You couldn't hear the rivers splashing down the weirs!

Wouldn't it be blank if you didn't have eyes?
You couldn't see the railway trains going down the lines!

Adam Kirkwood (10)
Eaglesfield Paddle CE (VA) Primary School

Wouldn't It Be Funny?

Wouldn't it be funny if you didn't have a nose?
You wouldn't be able to smell your stinky little toes.

Wouldn't it be boring if you didn't have your taste?
Your favourite Cadbury's chocolate would go to waste.

Wouldn't it be ghostly if you didn't have your touch?
Everything around you wouldn't feel like much.

Wouldn't it be quiet if you didn't have your ears?
You wouldn't be able to hear the bubbling froth on your beers.

Wouldn't it be blank if you didn't have eyes?
You wouldn't be able to see your tasty meat pies.

Jonathan Magrath (10)
Eaglesfield Paddle CE (VA) Primary School

Anger

Anger is red like a fierce exploding volcano
Anger tastes like anger coming into your body
Anger smells like burning hot water boiling in a pan
Anger feels like anger coming into your body and getting out
Anger sounds like people barking orders to their children
Anger looks into your body like bursting angry balloons
Anger reminds me of all the lovely things I have been through in my
life so far.

Lucy Pye (8)
Eaglesfield Paddle CE (VA) Primary School

Losing Your Senses

Wouldn't it be funny if you lost your nose?
You couldn't smell your stinky toes!

Wouldn't it be funny if you lost your taste?
All your chocolate ice cream would go to waste!

Wouldn't it be boring if you couldn't touch?
You couldn't hold the car clutch!

Wouldn't it be quiet if you couldn't hear?
You couldn't hear your mum yelling in your ear!

Wouldn't it be frightful if you didn't have your sight?
It would be like walking all the time in the middle of the night!

Ella Fanthorpe (10)
Eaglesfield Paddle CE (VA) Primary School

Anger

Anger is red like boiling blood running through my veins
Anger feels like hot boiling sun on my skin
Anger looks like a red-hot fire
Anger smells like an over-heated racing car
Anger tastes like the bitter taste of broccoli in my mouth
Anger reminds me of when my friend slapped me on my cheek.

Matthew Conway (7)
Eaglesfield Paddle CE (VA) Primary School

Sadness

Sadness
Sadness is blue like a deep blue sea running over the sand
Sadness
Sadness feels like a tear dropping from your eyes
Sadness
Sadness sounds like the music from the brown door of the ballroom
Sadness
Sadness tastes like the sour grapes my mum put in my lunchbox
Sadness
Sadness looks like the very last sweet in the box
Sadness
Sadness smells like the material on my least favourite jumper
Sadness
Sadness reminds me of the day my heart broke.

Sophie Douglas (7)
Eaglesfield Paddle CE (VA) Primary School

Anger

Anger is red like molten lava pouring out of volcanoes
Anger sounds like people shouting at you for being naughty
Anger tastes like red-hot scorching chilli powder burning in your mouth
Anger feels like you have lost all your possessions
Anger smells like the black smoke curling from a fire
Anger looks like flames from a dragon's nostrils
Anger reminds me of a being stuck in a giant traffic jam.

Rhys Kirkwood (7)
Eaglesfield Paddle CE (VA) Primary School

Happiness

Happiness is yellow like a burning hot sun
Happiness looks like the spring lambs jumping in the dusty grass
Happiness sounds like children's laughter in the playground
Happiness feels like the soft warm cuddles my mum gives me
Happiness tastes like the warm melting chocolate
Happiness smells like a fresh apple from a tree
Happiness reminds me of all the happy things I have done in my life.

Isy Drimmie (8)
Eaglesfield Paddle CE (VA) Primary School

Fear

Fear is black like a midnight sky
Fear looks like a cold blue sea whooshing through your body
Fear reminds me of strangers staring at the starry silver sky
Fear feels like an unhappy child living without a loving family
Fear smells like the cold damp Arctic
Fear tastes like the cold takeaway you ate last night.

Ella McGonigle (8)
Eaglesfield Paddle CE (VA) Primary School

Sadness

Sadness is blue like a dark ocean that never ends
Sadness reminds me of when my dog died
Sadness tastes like salty tears I've cried into my food
Sadness looks like a big rainfall coming from God's eyes
Sadness sounds like a puppy dog crying next to you
Sadness smells like dampness in the air.

Ciaran Ogilvie (7)
Eaglesfield Paddle CE (VA) Primary School

Anger

Anger is red like blood
Anger sounds like a person attacked by a tiger's jaw
Anger reminds me of my brother
Anger smells like a burnt piece of wood
Anger tastes like burnt cookies
Anger looks like an angry person
Anger feels like an angry person.

Dominique Cowley (8)
Eaglesfield Paddle CE (VA) Primary School

Love

Love is pink like a beautiful sunset
Love feels like a river of happiness
Love sounds like children laughing cheerily
Love smells like cold creamy ice cream
Love tastes like a heart-shaped biscuit
Love looks like a long pink river
Love reminds me of my family and friends.

Chloe Keenan-Wilson (7)
Eaglesfield Paddle CE (VA) Primary School

Sadness

Sadness is blue like a juicy blueberry
Sadness feels like a broken heart
Sadness looks like a roasted pheasant
Sadness tastes like the cry of a baby
Sadness sounds like the cry of an injured dove
Sadness smells like a blast of cold air
Sadness reminds me of friends I will never see again.

Daniel Vives Lynch (7)
Eaglesfield Paddle CE (VA) Primary School

Fear

Fear is white like a snowy mountain in the North Pole
Fear feels like you have just seen a ghost
Fear tastes like a prickly rose lying in a field
Fear sounds like a tiger sneaking up on its prey
Fear looks like a child with no family or someone to love them
Fear smells like the smoke rising from a just-fired shotgun
Fear reminds me of fearful heights.

Matthew Shepherd (8)
Eaglesfield Paddle CE (VA) Primary School

Anger

Anger is red like the burning lava from a volcano
Anger reminds me of revenge
Anger tastes like a flaming red-hot chilli fresh from the shop
Anger looks like the red sun setting
Anger sounds like a train beeping
Anger smells like black coal on a fire.

Keenan McDonald (8)
Eaglesfield Paddle CE (VA) Primary School

Love

Love is red like the heart in my body
Love feels like thinking of a loving pet
Love looks like you're staring dreamily
Love sounds like a stampeding herd
Love tastes like a fresh sweet strawberry
Love reminds me of my grandfather
Love smells like a sour, sweet, cherry bush.

Lucy Hammond (7)
Eaglesfield Paddle CE (VA) Primary School

Love

Love is red like a trickle of blood dripping out of your body
Love feels like you're sitting watching telly with your favourite
teddy bear
Love reminds me of my mum and dad getting married
Love smells like the sweet smell of dark chocolate
Love sounds like the romantic song in the country
Love tastes like the trickle of breadcrumbs falling into your mouth
Love looks like someone kissing.

Katy Livesey (7)
Eaglesfield Paddle CE (VA) Primary School

Love

Love is like a delicate red rose opening
Love reminds me of cuddling my brother in the morning
Love tastes like melting chocolate
Love feels like it will never end
Love sounds like church bells ringing
Love smells like perfume spreading in the air.

Abbie Louise Caine (8)
Eaglesfield Paddle CE (VA) Primary School

Love

Love is red like a heart beating quickly
Love feels like when you are warm and cosy in your bed
Love looks like the morning sunshine
Love sounds like songbirds singing on a beautiful summer morning
Love reminds me of my dog
Love tastes like chocolate with its own heart.

Harry Davies (8)
Eaglesfield Paddle CE (VA) Primary School

Happiness

Happiness is like spring and summer flowers in the green field
Happiness feels like your heart will never stop
Happiness smells like straw just being harvested
Happiness tastes like yellow buttercups flapping in the harvested
field nearby
Happiness reminds me of the good times playing with friends
Happiness looks like the love of your friends
Happiness sounds like a summer's day will never end.

Ewan Roberts (7)
Eaglesfield Paddle CE (VA) Primary School

Sadness

Sadness is blue like the deep blue sea
Sadness reminds me of when my dad goes away to work
Sadness feels like every day your life will never stop
Sadness sounds like wailing, crying whales from the ocean below
Sadness smells like the damp earth
Sadness looks like nothing but sadness
Sadness tastes like your heart has been broken.

Isla Campbell (8)
Eaglesfield Paddle CE (VA) Primary School

Hate

Hate is red and orange burning flames on a fire pit
Hate sounds like a giant *bang* of a fierce volcano erupting
Hate smells like burning toast
Hate looks like molten lava flowing down the rocky mountain
Hate feels like a slimy icy sea cucumber
Hate tastes like over-boiled Brussels sprouts
Hate reminds me of the Great Fire of London.

Adam Bainbridge (7)
Eaglesfield Paddle CE (VA) Primary School

Happiness

Happiness is yellow like the shining sun
Happiness smells like sunflowers flowing in the wind
Happiness feels like your best friend is coming to stay for the night
Happiness tastes like you're eating your favourite food
Happiness sounds like your friends are calling for you
Happiness looks like buttercups and daffodils growing
in the huge meadows
Happiness reminds me of the best times in my life.

Roisin Kingsbury (7)
Eaglesfield Paddle CE (VA) Primary School

Fear

Fear is red like the hot exploding fire
Fear reminds me of the hairy black spiders
Fear looks like a ginormous monster coming near you
Fear tastes like the disclosing tablets I have at the dentist
Fear sounds like the spooky ghosts howling in the wind
Fear feels like the wind touching your hair
Fear smells like the musty graveyard.

Christie Potts (7)
Eaglesfield Paddle CE (VA) Primary School

Happiness

Happiness is yellow like the golden sun
Happiness feels like I'm on holiday in America
Happiness looks like the smile on my face on Christmas Day
Happiness sounds like the bells on New Year's Eve
Happiness tastes like a sizzling pancake
Happiness smells like the spring daffodils
Happiness reminds me of waking up as a baby.

Kirsty Jayne Walker (7)
Eaglesfield Paddle CE (VA) Primary School

Sadness

Sadness is blue like a stretch of deep, dark sea
Sadness looks like small eddies in the wide sea
Sadness feels like big hurricanes in Pakistan
Sadness tastes like dead people in wars
Sadness sounds like people crying
Sadness smells like the damp soil
Sadness reminds me of Pippin and Tiggy, my old cats who have died.

Alannah Hambley (7)
Eaglesfield Paddle CE (VA) Primary School

Hate

Hate is red like the flowing lava
Hate looks like crashing meteors
Hate feels like the burning sun drying the earth
Hate smells like wood burning on a flaming fire
Hate sounds like an earthquake rattling the ground
Hate tastes like burning curry
Hate reminds me of a roaring fire.

Jordan Martin (8)
Eaglesfield Paddle CE (VA) Primary School

Night Comes

Night comes with sleepers snoring
Night comes with beds bouncing
Night comes with foxes barking
Night comes with badgers scratching
Night comes with moths fluttering
Night comes with bats flapping.

Archie Phillips (8)
Heversham St Peter's CE Primary School

Monster Poem

(Based on 'Jabberwocky' by Lewis Carroll)

Icy it was, as slushy snails slithered along frantically
Moans and grumbles heard from the gloomy forest
Naked were the trees up high
Suddenly silence had been struck.

'Beware, the Slapadash, my timid girl
His eyes are red, his fangs are white
When you creep across the endless wood
Take care my sweet bonny lass.'

Sian's red dagger was in hand ready to enter the forest
Her foe was nowhere in sight
So rested by the shlam, shlam pool
And sat awhile in wonder.

Crackles and crunches came from the wilderness wood
Out came the slushy Slapadash
Thumping on its way
The flaming red eyes twinkled in the moonlight.

Out came the glistening red dagger
The Slapadash slowly crept backwards
This was a sign of scaredness and shyness
They made friends and Sian went sprinting home.

'Come to me my brave girl
You have taught that monster a lesson
Hi, ho, hi, ho, what a glorious day,'
He beamed with happiness.

Icy it was, as slushy snails slithered along frantically
Moans and grumbles heard from the gloomy forest
Naked were the trees up high
Suddenly silence had been struck.

Francesca Ely (10)
Heversham St Peter's CE Primary School

Spikeopine

(Based on 'Jabberwocky' by Lewis Carroll)

Silence of the midnight air dazzling in the snow
Shone deeply on the shimmering icicles below.

'Beware the spikeopine, my son
The claws that burn, the jaws that turn
Fear the creature in the hot gleaming sun.'

He took his lethal dagger in his hand
And stabbed it in his gland
Making it screech and slither through the slime.

One, two, one, two, and through and through
The lethal dagger went deeply in
He left it dead as he fled.

Silence of the midnight air dazzling in the snow
Shone deeply on the shimmering icicles below.

Brendan Procter (10)
Heversham St Peter's CE Primary School

Sadness

Sadness sounds like someone crying
Sadness tastes like salty tears rolling down your face
Sadness smells bad like someone has hurt themselves
Sadness looks like someone being bullied
Sadness feels like gooey mush
I don't like being sad.

Elliot Handley (9)
Heversham St Peter's CE Primary School

Iceabop

(Based on 'Jabberwocky' by Lewis Carroll)

Dripping icicles waited to drop in the gruesome gloomy cave
Trees stood still in the piercing wind, glistening in the frost
Did crunch and crash, did splosh and splash in the cold cave
Suddenly a silence dawned over all the snowy land.

From the hideous cave crawled the Iceabop
His breath as cold as the North Pole, which will turn you
                                           into an ice block
His bellow can be heard from miles around and sounds
                                        like a clap of thunder
His body as long as the Great Wall of China and taller
                                          than a skyscraper.

She was not scared by an unfriendly monster
Instead of hiding in the opaque mist, she strode out from the fog
She lunged for the Iceabop and held out her sharp sword
She fought her way through the spiky thorns and saw a murky grotto.

Sneaking through the icy cave, a ghastly smell approached
Frosty icicles fell in front of her, smashing on the cold floor
Booming grunts and groans were heard from the end of the
                                              hideous dim cave
She edged to the back and peered round a pile of bones seeing
                                           a mangled shadow.

The Iceabop stood on his four feet and gave an ear-splitting roar
She stalked the enormous Iceabop careful not to hit his bulky
                                              prickly tail
Rapidly he saw her and shot his icy breath at her
Dodging the ice balls, she took out her threatening sword.

She sprinted behind the wicked monster, dashing round
                                            his revolting feet
Quickly she plunged her bold sword into the atrocious Iceabop
Blue blood came oozing out, the monster gave a tremendous growl
The Iceabop hit the solid rough ground and left there on that
                                           very bitter day.

Dripping icicles waited to drop, in the gruesome gloomy cave
Trees stood still in the piercing wind, glistening in the frost
Did crunch and crash, did splosh and splash in the cold cave
Suddenly a silence dawned over all the snowy land.

Didi Davies (10)
Heversham St Peter's CE Primary School

If I Was A Bully

If I was a bully, what would it be like?
Bursting a ball, breaking a bike.

If I was a bully, I'd make boys pay
By making them petrified in lunchtime play.

If I was a bully, I'd cheat in a race
By making everyone slip on some plaice.

If I was a bully, it would not be fair
Twisting your arm, pulling your hair.

If I was a bully, it would not be nice
By giving everyone some of my lice.

If I was a bully, it would not be cool
Making everyone look like a fool.

If I was a bully, it wouldn't be true
It's good I'm not a bully, just like you!

James Richards (9)
Heversham St Peter's CE Primary School

If I Was A Bully

If I was a bully
What would it be like?
Nicking a ball, breaking a bike.

If I was a bully
I would tell a lie
Kicking a teacher, making people cry.

If I was a bully
It wouldn't be fair
Nicking someone's bag, pulling someone's hair.

If I was a bully
It wouldn't be cool
Picking on little ones, making me rule.

Megan Carling (11)
Heversham St Peter's CE Primary School

A Recipe For Friendship

You need a tablespoon full of courage
Sieve in a pinch of belief
Beat in a cup of confidence
Add 100g of love
Mix in a teaspoon of trust
Stir in 250g of sharing
Beat in a cupful of support
Place it in the oven
Cut out a piece of kindness
And serve it with a smile.

Edward Pickthall (10)
Heversham St Peter's CE Primary School

Being Bullied

When the victim hasn't done anything
When the bully has done so many things
When the bully makes you mad
But you're too scared to tell Mum or Dad.

When you're being bullied
You want to scream and shout
Remember that you mustn't
Or the bully will catch you out!

When the bully is calling you names
Or they won't let you join in their games
When you don't want to go out and play
Because this bully is giving you a hard day.

Don't suffer in silence, just tell
If someone isn't treating you very well.

Ellie Taylor (9)
Heversham St Peter's CE Primary School

Illness

Illness is a slimy green colour
Illness tastes of disinfectant
Illness sounds like people being sick
Illness smells like the acidic smell of vomit
Illness looks like vegetable soup
Illness is slimy like a fish
Illness is worse than an elephant trumpeting down your ear.

Benedict Willacy (10)
Heversham St Peter's CE Primary School

Ackomoca

(Based on 'Jabberwocky' by Lewis Carroll)

A cold dark night in the dead desert
As the devilish Ackomoca roars
All living things running to hide
For this has happened before.

'Beware of Ackomoca, my son
It's time for him to hunt
Once he sees you, there's no turning back
His claws are never blunt
He will eat you, kill you
Or demolish anything in his sight
He doesn't care when he comes out of his lair
In the middle of the deep, dark night
You cannot see his steel-grey body
Or his shoulders as broad as a bus
But look in his eyes and he will immobilise
Each and every one of us.
The ground will tremble as he takes each step
And he smells like rotting tobacco
Don't go near unless you cut off his ear
With one terrible blow.'

Our hero is ready, Sir Hector Vival
With eyes darker than the bottom of the sea
With muscles so strong, it won't be long
Before Ackomoca is not free
Hector looks mean, he is always seen
With hair like a porcupine
He's as wise as an owl, sly as a fox
And always waits for the right time
To slay his foe, with one mighty blow
Sir Hector will certainly try
With arrow and bow, fighting he'll go
Like the greatest Samurai.

The battle begins at the mouth of the cave
And Ackomoca springs out,
To pounce on the knight
Who puts up a fight and lets out the loudest shout,
'Ackomoca, you devil, I'll stamp out your evil
You'll never win this fight
I'll cut off your ear and no one will fear you in the deep dark night.'
Ackomoca fights back with a sudden attack
And our hero falls to the floor

He gets up with a stagger and grabs his dagger
He is ready for more
The monster is stronger and the knight no longer
Ackomoca has won the battle
But what is the sound from underground
A mysterious rumbling rattle?
The beast looks down and with a frown turns over hero's hat
The bomb goes bang and with a clang
That was the end of that.

Will Jacques (10)
Heversham St Peter's CE Primary School

The Midnight Hero

(Based on 'Jabberwocky' by Lewis Carroll)

It was as dark as the midnight sky when the slithering frogs
Did the rustle in the trees
All miserable were the screeching parrots
When the moonlight cut across the lake.

'Beware of the monster, my son.'
The hero came from nowhere
A one, a two, a three, a punch, a kick, a bite
Then down, down, the grassy slope they did go.
Round and round like a dog chasing its tail
Then *thud,* They had reached the muddy base
The wings wrapped around the body
The warmth felt on the heart
My hero, my hero, my hero, you are my hero.

Charlotte Haddow (9)
Heversham St Peter's CE Primary School

Chopper

(Based on 'Jabberwocky' by Lewis Carroll)

The wind sloshed in the air
Night was a miserable one
The sky was as black as a jackdaw swooping in the sky.

'Beware of the Chopper, my son
The nails that scratch, the teeth that stab its prey
The eyes that stare
The Chopper, my son it's slimy and smelly
It's scaly and sticky
And it has a square button nose.

It has beady black eyes, three of them too
One for look-out, one for night vision
And one for seeing through you.'

They came for battle the Chopper and hero
The ground was wet and muddy
The hero was brave and strong.

The hero had blond hair to his shoulders
And had a shiny sword with blood from previous battles
And a shield, but he was no match against a monster.

The fight was bloody
The sword was clanging with the monster's thick, yellow fingernails
The smell of fear drifted through the cold air.

The hero was injured, blood pouring from a wound
He staggered over the uneven wet ground
And lay to take his last breath under the dark sky.

The wind sloshed in the air
Night was a miserable one
The sky was as black as a jackdaw in the sky.

Geroge Pickthall (10)
Heversham St Peter's CE Primary School

The Monster

(Based on 'Jabberwocky' by Lewis Carroll)

'Twas midnight and the forest trees
Did swish and sway in the breeze
All miserable was the atmosphere
And the creatures hid away.
'Beware the monster of the forest, my girl
The teeth that bite, the claws that kill.'

She took her weapons, sword, shield, net
And ventured out into the forest to hunt
Long time she posed and pondered
All at once, the monster teeth as sharp as skewers
Came charging through the tangled trees
Then suddenly stopped. It sat. It looked
And quite unexpectedly, it smiled and said,
'Hello . . . '

Nina Duxbury (10)
Heversham St Peter's CE Primary School

Death

Fear of death is black
Death sounds like bloodhounds flying at you
Death smells a horrible sooty stench
Death tastes grimy and musty
Death looks like your life flashing before your eyes
Death feels like nobody knows
Death must be lonely.

Ritchie Budd (10)
Heversham St Peter's CE Primary School

School Exits

Miss Rabbit's class bounced out
Mrs Elephant's herd stomped out
Mr Tiger's group ran out
Miss Pony's class trotted out
Mrs Cheetah's pack galloped out
Mr Bumble's group buzzed off
Miss Bull's class charged out
Mrs Bird's class fluttered out
Mr Kangaroo's herd leapt out
Miss Lizard's group crept out
Mrs Fairy's lot flew out
Mr Tarantula's group scattered out.

Abbie Thornley (7)
Heversham St Peter's CE Primary School

Happiness

Happiness is bright pink
It sounds like crystal clear water trickling gently down a stream
It smells like a warm loaf of bread baked freshly from the oven
It tastes like a creamy vanilla cupcake, sprinkled
with a touch of cinnamon
It looks like a little girl with red-rosy cheeks
After skipping gracefully across the dew-covered grass
Happiness is a glowing feeling deep inside your body
Happiness is *bright pink!*

Holly Watson (11)
Heversham St Peter's CE Primary School

School Exit Poem

Miss Antelope's lot fled out
Mr Bumble's lot buzzed off
Miss Cat's group purred out
Mr Dog's lot raced off
Miss Elephant's lot stomped out
Mr Frog's class hopped off
Miss Giraffe's children strolled out
Mr Horse's lot galloped off
Miss Iguana's class crawled out
Mr Jaguar's lot pounced off
Miss Kangaroo's children jumped out.

Bethany Clare (8)
Heversham St Peter's CE Primary School

Surprised

Surprised is a beaming bright yellow
It sounds like people doing clapping songs
Surprised smells like bread being made
It tastes like warm gingerbread men
Surprised looks like an amazing birthday cake
It feels like a crackling explosion
Surprised is a beaming bright yellow
I like being surprised!

Rachel Nield (10)
Heversham St Peter's CE Primary School

Newlands Valley

Animals grazing in the field
Brown, white, fluffy and soft
Crackling trees in the wind
Pointed mountains like party hats
A nearby house with smoke from its chimney
Going up and making a ghost-like fog
Autumn leaves sheltering the grass like a many-fingered hand
The trees like pencils in the landscape drawing
Shimmering grass as the sun shines down.

Megan Thornley (9)
Heversham St Peter's CE Primary School

Autumn Poem

Autumn comes with leaves rustling
Autumn comes with bonfires crackling
Autumn comes with fireworks banging
Autumn comes with hedgehogs crunching
Autumn comes with sweeping brushes
Autumn comes with bright orange colours
I like autumn.

Isabel Nield (8)
Heversham St Peter's CE Primary School

Rage

Rage is blood-red
Rage smells like rotten rubbish
Rage tastes like spicy red-hot curry
Rage looks like a blazing hot fire
Rage feels like a bubbling cauldron
Rage is blood-red.

Sophie Watson (9)
Heversham St Peter's CE Primary School

Windermere

Spiky trees waving in the breeze
Standing in a row like soldiers
Guarding the big blue lake
Mountains like long-necked dinosaurs
Spread across the horizon
Tiny fuzzy sheep graze
On the lush juicy grass
A castle in the distance
Peeps above the trees
I wonder who lives there.

Brendan McQue (8)
Heversham St Peter's CE Primary School

Rainforest Poem

Monkeys swinging through the trees
Always in packs of threes.

Snakes slithering along the ground
Catching their prey without a sound.

Tigers always on the prowl
If they see you, they might growl.

Birds always in their nests
And the little ones are sometimes pests!

Lauren Peers (9)
Heversham St Peter's CE Primary School

If Poem

If I become a horse
I will let you ride on me when you like.

If I become a wonderful whale
I will do lots of great tricks.

If I become a collie dog
I will do as I am told.

If I become a tall giraffe
I would let you climb on me.

If I become a beautiful white bird
I would let you chase me.

If I become a giant elephant
I would squirt you with water.

If I was a slow, slow snail
I would slither all over you.

But I am fine as I am!

Olivia Budd (9)
Heversham St Peter's CE Primary School

Night

Night comes with Simon's terrible music
Night comes with nightmares in the air
Night comes with typing on the computer
Night comes with medals clinking
Night comes with cars driving away
Night comes with cats miaowing
Sleep comes eventually.

Callum Cushnie (9)
Heversham St Peter's CE Primary School

Bridge In Wasdale

Thin, stony, grey, curved bridge
Arching over the beaming river
Shining and glimmering
Over the stones beneath
Like dragon's scales
Behind are
    Long
        Rocky
            Bumpy
                And grassy hills
Full of mazes
Ready for walkers to get lost in.

George Duxbury (8)
Heversham St Peter's CE Primary School

Skeleton

S kulls are like a rugby ball kicked up into the air
K nees are like a mountain with black snow on top
E lvis the Pelvis wiggles his hips like a snake
L ivers are like purple rubbers
E ars are like bumpy bowls
T eeth are like a very sharp knife
O rgans are like pink juicy oranges
N oses are like a right-angle triangle.
    That's a skeleton!

Thomas Moses (8)
Heversham St Peter's CE Primary School

If

If I become a wolf
I will howl in your ear.

If I become a lion
I would eat you up.

If I become a cat
I would cuddle you a lot.

If I become a chicken
I would lay you lots of eggs.

If I become a pink flamingo
I would balance on one leg.

If I become a slimy frog
I would hop around all day.

If I become a fiery dragon
I would breathe fire in your face.

But I'm just happy . . . being me!

Jody Tideswell (7)
Heversham St Peter's CE Primary School

Skeleton

S kull is like the moon with two craters
K nee is like a big solid rock
E lbow is like a meteorite moving in and out
L eg is like a long bendy tower
E ach ear is like a massive hold
T ibia is like a long white sword
O rgans are like squidgy jelly
N eck bone is like a long hard snake.

Tom Taylor (8)
Heversham St Peter's CE Primary School

Crummock Water

Sky like water in the air
Reflecting everywhere
Hills like hard hats
With scarcely a sound
Spoiling their sunbeamed brims
Which gleam daily till daylight dims
Golden bushes like syrup on the ground
Surrounding the super lake
Glimmering
Rippling
All around.

Rob Calland (9)
Heversham St Peter's CE Primary School

Spring Comes

Spring comes with birds singing
Spring comes with lambs bleating
Spring comes with chickens clucking
Spring comes with cockerels cock-adoodle-doodling
Spring comes with dogs woofing
Spring comes with pigs snorting
Spring comes with children laughing
Spring comes to warm you up
I love spring.

Hannah Douthwaite (8)
Heversham St Peter's CE Primary School

Alphabet Haunted Castle

A is for argh, alarmed and afraid
B is for boo, banshees and beasts
C is for creaking and coffins
D is for dark and dangerous dungeons
E is for eek and eerie eyeballs
F is for fear and foxes
G is for ghosts and ghouls
H is for horror and hungry hounds
I is for ice and icicles hanging down
J is for joints jittering
K is for killing with a knife
L is for laughing in the loft
M is for magic and mystery at midnight
N is for noise and naughty nights
O is for omens and opening doors
P is for phantoms poking around
Q is for quick and quiet queens
R is for rascal rat
S is for spectres and snakes
T is for troublesome toads
U is for UFOs hiding underground
V is for vampires vanishing
W is for werewolves wandering
X is for X-ray eyes
Y is for yelling
Z is for zombies and zapping.

Joshua Rushton (8)
Heversham St Peter's CE Primary School

Spooky Poem

A is for argh!
B is for boo
C is for crocodiles killing canaries
D is for deadly Dracula
E is for a hypnotised elephant
F is for fangless Frankenstein
G is for growing ground monster
H is for a howling hill
I is for ice monster
J is for Japanese monster
K is for killer kangaroo
L is for Loch Ness monster
M is for monstrous man
N is for nightmare
O is for overnight octopus
P is for perfect prowler
Q is for queuing monster
R is for roaring dinosaur
S is for slimy snake
T is for tall pterodactyl
U is for ugly Uranium monster
V is for vindictive monster
W is for wailing wind
X is for xylophone monster
Y is for yelling monster
Z is for zapping monster.

John Hodgkinson (9)
Heversham St Peter's CE Primary School

Skeleton

S kull is like a hard professional football balancing on your neck
K nee is like a hard-boiled egg that's unbreakable
E lbow is like a piece of rock always getting bashed
L ungs are like marshmallows going in and out
E ar is like a home for ants
T oes are like wriggly worms wriggling about
O rgans are like purple, fat, juicy things
N oses are like a sharp piece of slate with holes in it.
A skeleton!

Daniel Dixon (8)
Heversham St Peter's CE Primary School

That's Me!

I am a comfy pillow that is as soft as can be
I am a bumpy apple that's the right size for your hands
I am as pink as your skin that's also the same as a rose
I am a sly cat that pinches the best seat
I am a snowdrop as white as the snow
I am an Olympic swimmer that's very fast
But I am Trudi, that's me!

Trudi Beuzeval (9)
Heversham St Peter's CE Primary School

Night

Night comes with babies crying
Night comes with bats flying
Night comes with people snoring
Night comes with beds creaking
Night comes with water dripping
Night comes with peacocks coughing.

Dennis Dixon (8)
Heversham St Peter's CE Primary School

School Exit Poem

Mr Firework's class boomed out
Mr Chicken's group clucked off
Mr Laughing's lot giggled out
Mr Saw's class soared out
Miss Mouse's lot scuttled off
Mr Bullet's lot fired out
Mr Worms' class wriggled off
Mr Swimmer's group swam out
Mr Bee's lot buzzed out.

Ben Heseltine (7)
Heversham St Peter's CE Primary School

School Exit Poem

Mr Plane's class soared out
Miss Dog's lot raced out
Mr Pig's lot trotted out
Miss Elephant's lot stomped out
Mr Horse's lot galloped out
Miss Duck's lot quacked out
Mr Slug's lot slithered out
Miss Cheetah's lot shot out.

Oliver Somers (9)
Heversham St Peter's CE Primary School

When Assembly Finished

Mr Bumble's lot buzzed off
Mr Bap's lot rolled off
Mr Hop's lot hopped off
Mr Spider's lot webbed their way out
Mr Pig's gang ate their way out
Mr Army's gang shot their way out
Mr Chainsaw's gang chopped a way out
And Mr Lazy's lot got carried out!

Adam Lynch (8)
Heversham St Peter's CE Primary School

Class Exodus

Miss Snail's class all slimed out
Mr Mole's lot dug their way out
Mrs Mouse's children scampered out
Miss Salmon's lot swam out
Mr Snake's children wiggled out
Mrs Kangaroo's class hopped out
Home time!

Cameron Blood (9)
Heversham St Peter's CE Primary School

The Magic Box

(Based on 'Magic Box' by Kit Wright)

I will put in the box . . .
The shine of a sparkly headband ready for a party,
Singing birds on a lovely oak tree,
Stars on a bright night.

I will put in the box . . .
A glass of water with magic paintbrushes,
A cute, shy puppy,
A monkey having a party.

I will put in the box . . .
Me and my friends that are kind and lovely,
A big cave as black as night,
A teacher with a remote and a child with a pen.

My box is fashioned with . . .
A chocolate handle,
Some jewels and diamonds for hinges
And loads of sweets.

My box is fashioned from sparkly fabric with stars on it,
Some lovely deserts
And a picture of me.

I surf on my box over a high mountain
Which touches the sky and I will land in my room.

Georgia Cooper (8)
Holy Family Catholic School

Cat

All cats . . .

Abandoned cats in streets
Wild cats in Australia
Pet cats in houses
Big cats in Africa
Wild cats in woods
All sorts of cats
Leopards, lions, tigers, house cats and abandoned cats
How many cats in the world?
I have a cat called Charlie
And he is the same as any other cat
Cats have fur
Long fur
Short fur
Big fur
Little fur
How much fur?

Anna Roberts (8)
Holy Family Catholic School

Elizabeth

E lizabeth loves chatting
L ikes chocolate
I s a big sister to Victoria
Z ebras are not her favourite animal
A pples are her favourite fruit
B abies are cute
E lizabeth loves school
T eachers teach Elizabeth to learn
H olidays are fun.

Elizabeth Morgan (8)
Holy Family Catholic School

The High School Musical Box

(Based on 'Magic Box' by Kit Wright)

I will put in the box . . .
Chad cheering cheerleaders
Taylor shooting hoops
Sharpay dressing up.

I will put in the box . . .
Gabriella dancing along
Troy practising the musical
Chelsea playing pianos.

I will put in the box . . .
Wildcat mascots
Troy and Gabriella meeting
Sharpay spying on them.

I will put in the box . . .
Taylor having her way
Chad getting his head in the game
Mrs Darbus shouting in rage.

I will put in the box . . .
Chelsea writing songs
Ryan listening to Sharpay
Sharpay bossing Ryan about.

I will put in the box . . .
Gabriella doing experiments
Troy sweating like mad
Chelsea against Ryan.

My box is fashioned with royal photos
And rubies on it.

Emily Russell (7)
Holy Family Catholic School

My Magic Box

(Based on 'Magic Box' by Kit Wright)

I will put in the box . . .
A crown with sparkling marshmallows,
A candy cane,
The pop of popcorn.

I will put in the box . . .
A soft pillow of candyfloss,
A dairy milk bar.

My box has got marshmallows all around
And its hinges are sparkly.

I will fly on my box to the North Pole to meet Santa.
I will press a button to land on a pink land.

Tamsyn Duff (7)
Holy Family Catholic School

Ten Things Found In A Clown's Pocket

A letter from his mum saying, *don't forget the juggling trick.*
A big, red, squeaking nose.
A flower that squirts water!
A big, curly, orange wig.
Lots of laughing people.
A trapeze.
A one-wheeled bike.
Big, red, rosy cheeks.
A big grey cannon
Lots of paint to decorate his face.

And that's what you'll find in a clown's pocket.

Jacob McSweeney (7)
Holy Family Catholic School

Ten Things Found In A Cat's Pocket

A fat, shining fish.
A dirty and muddy claw.
A glittering and sparkling paw print.
A cut piece of pink wool.
A grey and white whisker.
A black and white hair.
A big, dark shadow.
A dead mouse
A crumpled leaf
And a cute picture of her kitten.

Jennifer Singleton (7)
Holy Family Catholic School

Ten Things Found In A Knight's Pocket

A gleaming mask.
A yellow feather.
A dazzling gleaming dagger.
A crown.
A suit of armour.
A sock.
A tissue
A puppet.
Some handcuffs and
Some jewellery.

Lewis Singleton (7)
Holy Family Catholic School

My Family

L ydia is a chocoholic.
Y oghurt is her favourite item.
D ad eats too many cream eggs.
I eat bananas.
A nd Mum loves Dad.

Tommy Robertson (8)
Holy Family Catholic School

Ten Things Found In A Fairy's Pocket

A sparkling dress.
A magical super wand.
A rare beautiful crown.
Sapphire and ruby jewels in a box.
Red, shiny, high-heeled shoes.
A golden ring given by a prince.
A billion dollars.
A silver coat.
A diamond bracelet.
Ruby earrings.

Sophie Edmondson (8)
Holy Family Catholic School

The Alien's Box

I will put in the box . . .
A sparkling flying saucer
A Russian dog
Half the moon
Five gleaming stars
Ben10 aliens
A laser gun for the aliens
A few dead bodies
An army man in a flying saucer
An alien in an army tank.

William Martin (8)
Holy Family Catholic School

Wands

W izards have us,
A nd so do witches,
N o one else can
D o the magic that we can do,
S o leave the magic to the professionals!

Hannah Alarakia-Charles (7)
Holy Family Catholic School

Five Things Found In A Witch's Pocket

A big black spider that creeps about at night.
A black pointed hat that glows very brightly.
A rat that squeaks and squiggles.
A big black bat that sings in the night,
And a big shiny wand.

That's what you will find in a witch's pocket.

Sophie Shannon (7)
Holy Family Catholic School

Five Things Found In A Cat's Pocket

A ball of wool, stringy and short,
A soft gentle purr that's careful,
A big miaow that drifts through the house,
A fat fabulous fish,
Some super sparkly whiskers.

These are five things found in a cat's pocket.

Amy Simpson (8)
Holy Family Catholic School

Tamsyn

T amsyn loves sweets
A nd she loves playing
M ost games with me
S o, so small
Y ou're so, so cute
N oisy Tamsyn!

Maria Guselli (8)
Holy Family Catholic School

Seven Things Found In Stevie G's Pocket

A brand new football,
£2,000,
A Liverpool necklace,
And a Liverpool annual,
A picture of his wife,
A shiny medal,
And a Liverpool flag.

Alfie Murphy (8)
Holy Family Catholic School

Money

Money is fine.
Money is divine.
Money is green.
Money is mean.
Money is wacky.
Money is tacky.
Money is my favourite thing *whoo!*

Morgan Hulston (8)
Holy Family Catholic School

The Cyclops' Revenge

Hear me ocean floors,
Make them suffer, get them, have them for your supper.
Maker of the storms so deep!
Great god of the sea animals that creep,
Send me piranhas, send me rain,
Send me darkness, send them pain,
Send me storms too heavy
For the skies to contain!
May wasps swarm,
Sting with your power,
Close round Odysseus and his fine men,
May they get whiplash,
May they get stings to the mass,
May they never see their wives again!

Lisa Holme (11)
Orton CE School

The Cyclops' Revenge

Hear me sea creatures
Great stings, water wizards
Fabulous storms and floods make
Great god of the ocean!
Send me thunder, send me lightning
Send me volcanoes too light
For the sky to contain!
May the wind blow and hiss
With your stinging
Close round Odysseus
And his fine men;
May they wreck their ships
May they never set foot
On their own lands again!

Bethany Woof (11)
Orton CE School

The Cyclops' Revenge

Hear me storm of all seas
Wave maker, killer, wind blower
Great god of the dark.
Send me waves, send me wind
Send me rain, lightning
Send me dark for the skies to contain.
May birds sing with your anger
Close around Odysseus and his fine men.
May they drown
May they die
May they never set foot on their own land
Again.

Charlotte Whitham (10)
Orton CE School

Giraffe

Inside the giraffe's leg, the long tree
Inside the long tree, the giraffe's neck
Inside the giraffe's neck, the river flows
Inside the river flows, the giraffe's spiky hair
Inside the giraffe's spiky hair, snow falling
Inside snow falling, the giraffe's tail
Inside the giraffe's tail, the long snake
Inside the long snake, the giraffe's hoof
Inside the giraffe's hoof, animals run
Inside animals run, the giraffe's long leg.

Courtney Wearmouth (11)
Orton CE School

Amulet

Inside the whale's call, the deepest depth of ocean.
Inside the deepest depth of ocean, the gentle appearance.
Inside the gentle appearance, the swift sea.
Inside the swift sea, the peaceful sigh.
Inside the peaceful sigh, the beam of heavenly light.
Inside the beam of heavenly light, the whale's wish for life.
Inside the whale's wish for life, the sudden danger.
Inside the sudden danger, the whale's high-pitched warning.
Inside the whale's high-pitched warning, the bobbing boat.
Inside the bobbing boat, the cry of terror.
Inside the cry of terror, the bloodthirsty fishermen.
Inside the bloodthirsty fishermen, the last breath.
Inside the last breath, a new life.
Inside a new life, the whale's call.

Tessa Ellen Higgs (11)
Orton CE School

The Gibbons

Inside the drawn-out arms, the boughs of trees.
Inside the boughs of trees, the gibbons swinging.
Inside the gibbons swinging, the grasping hands.
Inside the grasping hands, the fruit's juices.
Inside the fruit's juices, the moist forest's depths.
Inside the moist forest's depths, the clamorous calling.
Inside the clamorous calling, the branches plummeting,
Inside the branches plummeting, the cheeky laughter.
Inside the cheeky laughter, the males duelling.
Inside the males duelling, the drawn-out arms.

Emma Elizabeth Barker (10)
Orton CE School

Inside The Lion

Inside the lion's sharp-clawed paws, the river of blood.
Inside the river of blood, the gleaming eye.
Inside the gleaming eye, the tear from the boar.
Inside the tear from the boar, the crafty lion.
Inside the crafty lion, the death of another.
Inside the death of another, the kill of a lion.
Inside the kill of a lion, the dangerous teeth of the king.
Inside the dangerous teeth of the king, the pounce of a young one.
Inside the pounce of a young one, the cry of a mother.
Inside the cry of a mother, the night stars.
Inside the night stars, the fierce touch of the beast.
Inside the fierce touch of the beast, the cry of a stray.
Inside the cry of a stray, the lion's sharp-clawed paws.

Jenny Coates (10)
Orton CE School

Amulet

Inside the hawk's shining eyes, the sun's reflection
Inside the sun's reflection, the hawk's golden wings
Inside the hawk's golden wings, the summer winds
Inside the summer winds, the hawk's deadly talons
Inside the hawk's deadly talons, the rat's scream
Inside the rat's scream, the silent night
Inside the silent night, the hawk's cry
Inside the hawk's cry, the still grass
Inside the still grass, the hawk's nest
Inside the hawk's nest, the rat's tail
Inside the rat's tail, the screaming chicks,
Inside the screaming chicks, the icy wind
Inside the icy wind, the hawk's shining eyes.

Mark Potter (10)
Orton CE School

Adventures Of Emily

Emily met an ugly pig
Emily, Emily, did a jig
The pig was hungry, the pig was fat
The pig was spotty and had a cat
The pig said, 'Glad to see you
How do you do? Now I shall eat you.'
Emily, Emily, never did worry
Emily never did scream or scurry
She threw her special bunny
And turned the pig into runny honey.

Emily Pinder (9)
Orton CE School

Tiger

Inside the tiger's excellent sneaking, the deadly darting.
Inside the deadly darting, the roasting terrain.
Inside the roasting terrain, the slim body.
Inside the slim body, the streaky back.
Inside the streaky back, the dim jungle.
Inside the dim jungle, the dry tongue.
Inside the dry tongue, the struggling gazelle.
Inside the struggling gazelle, the bleak eyes.
Inside the bleak eyes, the excellent sneaking.

George Mason (10)
Orton CE School

Red Kite Circle

Inside the kite's wild wings, the soft speed.
Inside the kite's soft speed, the fire-red feathers.
Inside the fire-red feathers, the dark red eyes.
Inside the dark red eyes, a pair of claws
Inside the pair of claws, two rats' bodies.
Inside two rats' bodies, the kite's beak.
Inside the kite's beak, the cry of a rat.
Inside the cry of a rat, the rat's family.
Inside the rat's family, the wild wings.

Keenan Bentley-Todd
Orton CE School

The Leopard

Inside the leopard's claw is the dead zebra.
Inside the dead zebra is the leopard's face.
Inside the leopard's face is the leopard's fur.
Inside the leopard's fur are the leopard's feet.
Inside the leopard's feet is the leopard's paw.
Inside the leopard's paw is the rocky path.
Inside the rocky path are the little bugs.
Inside the little bugs are the leopard's claws.

Harry Laidlow (11)
Orton CE School

The Hot, Sunny Beach

T he hot warm beach as you walk across the sand.
H ot sunny day at the beach.
E ach holiday you run to the beach and enjoy the beach.

S parkling sea when it comes up to your feet.
U nder rocks you see crabs moving left and right.
N asty seagulls flying by.
N aughty people dropping litter.
Y oung babies making sandcastles.

H ard rocks as grey as the moon.
O ctopuses coming to shore and tickling you.
T alking adults never stop on the beach.

B oats going to shore.
E ating a picnic on the beach is fun!
A ccidents can happen on the beach.
C rabs biting people's toes.
H olidays are so much fun on the beach.

Catherine Gorry-Edwards (9)
Roose Primary School

The Waves

T he gigantic waves.
H ere at the beach it's nice and lovely.
E veryone is happy here.

W aves crashing, in the water splashing people.
A ccepting the sun
V olume of the sea is very loud
E veryone is screaming
S o people put earmuffs on.

Samuel McDonald (9)
Roose Primary School

The Boisterous Bubbling Beach

The sun is shining on the sand,
And I can see all the beach's land,
I can hear the waves gently crashing,
I can also see the shells sadly smashing.

People digging sandcastles just for fun,
Whilst they sit in the boiling hot sun,
The sea is blue like the sky,
Lots of people walking by.

The trees are green and very tall,
The waves are crashing over the wall,
Fish swim to the water's edge,
People hiding behind a hedge.

Jake Carter (9)
Roose Primary School

The Glamorous Gleaming Seaside

Everyone's waiting for you at the sunny seaside.
The waves are crashing and smashing and it's really, really wide.
The sparkling sand and the ginormous whales float.
I wonder what they eat.
I think it's slimy sloppy snails.

Joshua Singleton (8)
Roose Primary School

The Extreme Beach

The crashing waves rush to the shore.
Seagulls screaming *more, more, more!*
The stormy sky goes *crash, crash, crash,*
The waves on the rocks go *smash, smash, smash!*

Amelia Bird (8)
Roose Primary School

The Hip Hop Beach

T he ripping, rocking roaring sea,
H iding away, not seeing me,
E ver active, waves flying high.

H ipping, hopping light blue sky,
I mpact, flying in the air with glee.
P opping up with little fishes.

H opping across the sandy land.
O pen fields, very bland.
P inning someone in its grasp.

B opping around, washing seaweed.
E ating stuff as it comes along.
A shark! It's eating fishes.
C 'mon everyone! Let's have a picnic and eat those dishes!
H ey everyone, let's go fishing!

Joe McCormick   (8)
Roose Primary School

Frightening Fierce Beach

The beach can give you a scare,
If you jump out at a bear.

The waves splash,
As you bash.

The beach is scary,
My name is Mary.

Chloe Barrow (8)
Roose Primary School

What People Do At The Beach

Some might go to the hot dog stand
Maybe others stroll across the squashy sand.
Lots of people swim in the sea,
To keep out of the sun people sit under the palm tree.

Waves crash and bang against the rocks,
While people take off their socks.
The sky shines from above,
There in the sky flies a peaceful dove.

As the dolphins jump up and down,
People dig and lots of stuff is found.
All the children splash and play,
Then their mum says, 'Let's pack away!'

Joshua Woodend (9)
Roose Primary School

Sea Creatures

Under the sea where sea creatures live,
There lives a crab and a crab it is.

Under the sea where sea creatures live,
There is a rainbowfish which is very colourful.

Under the sea where sea creatures live,
There is an octopus with eight long legs.

Matthew Tongue (9)
Roose Primary School

The Sparkling Beach

The sparkling sea moving past,
The waves moving very fast.

Boiling hot sun for the view,
Where will you lie that depends on you?

The sun gleaming on the sand,
Will it cover the whole land?

All the fish swimming around,
Will they swim down to the ground?

All the shells in the water,
All the palm trees getting shorter.

Francesca Barry (8)
Roose Primary School

Tiger

Meat lover
Prey catcher
Teeth sinker
Blood drinker
Good stalker
Teeth lasher
Tree climber
Claw scratcher
Good leaper
Eye watcher
Jungle survivor
Fast mover.

Jenny Rothery (10)
Rosley CE Primary School

Tigers

Grass disguiser,
Black striper,
Coat hunted,
Carnivorous eater,
Blood drinker,
Organ ripper,
No mercy,
Sharp toother,
Long leaper,
Fast runner,
Glassy eyer,
Jungle lover!

Owen Cundall (9)
Rosley CE Primary School

Dolphin

Shark teaser
Fish eater
Fast swimmer
Fish stealer
Ocean lover
Water glider
Good diver
Long noser
Big jumper
Long swimmer.

Rosie Groves (10)
Rosley CE Primary School

Snow Leopard

Snowy predator,
Born anger,
Goat muncher,
Rabbit ripper,
Quiet mover,
Snow shuffler,
Grey thunder,
Rapid decreaser.

Guy Rodger (10)
Rosley CE Primary School

Clouds

The clouds are fluffy, just like a puppy,
The clouds are running around the world,
The clouds are big and small just like a puppy!
Clouds are round and thin and so are puppies!

The clouds are like a rainbow after rain,
Clouds change colour because of the light.
They can be pink in the morning or evening,
The clouds can be orange like a flame!

Clouds can be any shape or size.
They can be like Winnie the Pooh or a fish,
Or a person or a cat or a plate,
They can change shape in your imagination!

Clouds are destructive and violent,
They can hold lightning and thunder,
They can hold water, water makes rivers overflow,
Clouds can hold hail and wind and snow!

Benedict Shackleford, Timothy Dixon, Kayley Sharp,
Andalucia Armstrong-Squires, Bernadette Thompson,
Shay Tinnion (9) & Annie Rebecca Gardner (8)
St Joseph's Catholic Primary School, Cockermouth

Clouds

C louds can be your enemy or friend,
    you might not survive to the end,
    like a fluffed blanket itching to be touched,
    watch you don't rely on them too much.

L ooking down at the world's deep end,
    I really hope clouds will be my friend,
    Listening down at every conversation ever made,
    We can't live without clouds as our friend.

O nly one touch, you fall back down to reality,
    We live on Earth, they live in the sky,
    I know one thing for a fact, clouds will never die.

U nderneath them, I know clouds will watch over me,
    When I die, I hope I'll join them,
    Floating free in another universe,
    Just waiting to be seen.

D own on Earth I know I can always depend on clouds,
    Wherever I go, they guide me,
    Into two universes, I'm the only one who knows.

S o I'll look forward to joining them,
    But first I'll live my life on Earth,
    But the clouds will always come first.

Anna Helen Heywood (11)
St Joseph's Catholic Primary School, Cockermouth

Clouds

Big black clouds,
Looking cold and destructive,
Taking over the sky!
The big, black, dark clouds are threatening.
The scary clouds are going to give a big, big storm.
There are going to be floods all over the place!

Kai Cartwright (10)
St Joseph's Catholic Primary School, Cockermouth

Clouds

Clouds can come in all shapes and sizes
Like plates made of snow
Or snow animals in the sky,
The clouds will never die.

Clouds swiftly move across the sky
Like planes flying in the big sky.
Clouds are beautiful, big and small,
The clouds will never die!

Clouds of all colours in the sunset,
The clouds have a big rest,
So they will always look their best!
The clouds will never die!

Clouds can be your enemy or your friend,
They are there until the end.
The clouds will always live in the sky.
The clouds will never die!

Jonathan Peter Broad (10)
St Joseph's Catholic Primary School, Cockermouth

Clouds

Big, white and fluffy
Small, thin and wispy.
Big cushions dotted around the sky,
A massive blanket of candyfloss covering the world.

Floating around in the sky
Changing colours every day.
In the night they bring a friend,
Which flashes every second.

When the sun starts to set
They will make a lovely picture.
The colours come out and start to change,
Pink, blue, yellow, black and purple.

Clouds can be anything you want
Any shape and size.
Any colour you want,
Just find your imagination.

Jacinta Ryan (10)
St Joseph's Catholic Primary School, Cockermouth

Clouds

Clouds are stunning
And change to what you want.
They look like snow
And can be pink, purple, white and black.

Clouds can move with the wind
And are as soft as a cushion.
All shapes and sizes,
Smooth, rough and rugged.

You can lose them behind the mountains
And you will see them
When the wind blows them back.
They can be powerful or polite.

They can be dark at night and bright at day.
Big ones, little ones,
But never will they be the same.

Daniel Curry (9)
St Joseph's Catholic Primary School, Cockermouth

Clouds

Clouds can be dangerous.
Clouds do not bring much atmosphere.
They can be very scary.
Dark clouds are not pleasant.

Clouds can look like a rainbow.
They are very colourful.
Clouds can be beautiful.
They are soft and fluffy.

Clouds can be different shapes!
They can look like a big circle.
They sometimes look like big plates,
Clouds can look like a big bed.

The colour of clouds is lovely.
The colour of clouds is sunny.
At night clouds can look like the moon.
At night clouds can look sleepy.

Eweline Zmuda (9)
St Joseph's Catholic Primary School, Cockermouth

Clouds

Clouds are fluffy, clouds are white,
They look really nice during the night.
White fluffy clouds, soft as a puppy,
Clouds are desire in vivid colours of fire.

Dark clouds in the sky,
Miserable things really high.
Thunder, lightning, they are so frightening!
Why are they big? Why aren't they small?
I wouldn't want to be very tall.

Different shape, different size,
They attract you if you do exercise.
Sometimes they shock you,
Too bright for your eyes,
But they always give you a big surprise.

Now you see what clouds can be when you walk by,
Clouds are great,
But I don't want them on my plate.
But if you want to see what clouds can be,
You're in for a big surprise!

Lauren Sian Coulson (8)
St Joseph's Catholic Primary School, Cockermouth

Clouds

Clouds can be really fluffy,
Clouds can be really smooth too,
Clouds are like big bags of cotton wool,
Clouds are pink, orange and yellow on sunsets.

Clouds can come in different shapes and sizes,
Clouds can be anything you want them to be,
Even on a rainbow, you'll see!

Charlotte Gardner (10)
St Joseph's Catholic Primary School, Cockermouth

Clouds

Clouds can be different shapes,
Clouds make me feel that I can fly,
Some clouds are rolled up in circles like tape,
When I see no clouds I sigh.

Some clouds can be pink,
Some clouds can shine,
Sometimes clouds sink,
Sometimes clouds go in lines.

Some clouds are really fluffy,
Sometimes clouds look like mountaintops,
Some clouds are really puffy,
Sometimes clouds never stop.

When I look at clouds, they're white,
A second later they'll be bright,
Some clouds can grow and grow,
Some clouds look like snow!

Edward Meek
St Joseph's Catholic Primary School, Cockermouth

Clouds

Clouds can come in all different shapes,
They can look like white snow-covered animals,
Or transport vehicles.

They can also be in strange colours for clouds,
Such as, orange, red, white,
Purple and pink.

Clouds can be humongous
To a tiny little snowdrop,
Or a little bit of cotton wool.

The clouds are water vapour,
This is in the water cycle.
They are at their most beautiful,
When the sun is setting.

Athie Armstrong-Squires (10)
St Joseph's Catholic Primary School, Cockermouth

Free

It came crashing down,
I didn't know what to do,
Everybody screamed and ran,
I went with them.

My heart pounded,
I didn't know where I was going,
More bombs cascaded down,
I scuttled down the dark streets.

Soon I was out in the countryside,
The birds singing in the trees,
The sun beaming on the open air,
All I knew was that I was free!

Sam Styan (8)
Staveley Primary School

My Mum Ate . . .

My mum ate . . .

a popped football with lots of holes
and a piece of mud with lots of moles.

My mum ate . . .

A wet paper towel with lots of creases
and a big black coat with lots of fleeces.

My mum ate . . .

A very sharp pencil with lots of rubbers
and a big red pub with lots of clubbers.

Eddy Hubble (7)
Staveley Primary School

Seasons

Winter is cold and it is very chilly sledging down the hill.
Spring is very beautiful with all those flowers blooming in the sun
And every flower has a different colour.
Summer is hot and you go swimming at the beach
And make sandcastles.
Autumn leaves falling all around in different colours
Going round and round in different patterns.

Adam Baker-Ellwood (7)
Staveley Primary School

My Family

My mum is kind because she helps me with hard homework
My dad is funny because he makes up funny rhymes
My sisters are helpful because they help me do my laces
My brother is a little annoying because he gets out of bed and
switches the light on.
My cat is a hunter. She hunts the mice and eats them.
My family is loving and kind.

Oliver Jackson (7)
Staveley Primary School

My Family

My family is helpful because they do things for me
My family never picks their noses
My family is nice to people who they don't know
My family never spends a lot of money
My family is so cool
My family never burps without going out of the room.

Kieran Raven (8)
Staveley Primary School

My Friends

Amy is my best friend
It is Amy because she never gives up
She is always there for me when there is something up
She is big into friendship.

Joanne is a good friend
Sweet and nice
When it comes to writing a poem she always gives advice
She is neat at writing
She never leaves me behind.

Ellie is a good friend
I will tell you why
She is very excited
Do you know why?
She will let you play in every game
And not leave you behind.

Connie is a good friend too
She is sweet and kind
She has good reasoning
And a brilliant mind.

Jordan is really kind
She is new at the school
But fits in very nicely.

Robyn Bowness (7)
Staveley Primary School

My Pets

M y pets are lovely, I love them so much.
  I have got guinea pigs, they are really squeaky.

Y ou will think they are lovely so come and see them.
  I have got hamsters, my one is a girl, she is really cute.

P ets are one thing that you have to look after
  and clean out their enormous cages. I have got chickens,
  they lay loads of eggs and they make a lot of noise.

E ach type of animal has its own cage. I have got cats,
  they are really miaowy and are obviously very beautiful.

T eatime is their favourite time because they love their food.
  I have got dogs, they are really cute and woofy.

S et off on a holiday, they all hate that but we always care for them
  when we go. Just one more thing, I love them all!

Joanne Smith (7)
Staveley Primary School

Sweets

Chocolate fudge, marshmallow and gobstoppers.
Yummy sweets for me.

Tummy's rumbling for yummy, yummy sweets.

Sherbet lemon just for me
And sticky toffee pudding too.

Tummy's rumbling for yummy, yummy sweets.

Lovely double chocos, Coco Pops and Poppets.

Tummy's rumbling for yummy, yummy sweets
And that tummy is mine.

Millie Whitehead (8)
Staveley Primary School

Out Of This World I Will Find . . .

Out of this world I will find . . .
A rusty smashed UFO
Some alien droppings
A never-stopping light
An alien Sumo wrestler

Out of this world I will find . . .
Mars with a cascading river.

Oliver Clegg (8)
Staveley Primary School

Winter

W inter is all snowy, lots of sledges racing down a hill.

I n winter all the big gusts and snowy winds give me a chill.

N ow I'm going out to play on my Santa sleigh.

T oday I saw a polar bear skiing down Mount Everest to
Death Valley.

E lephants ice-skating, such a strange sight to see.

R eappearing aliens going to and fro, laughing at each other.

Isabel Cambray (8)
Staveley Primary School

Dinosaurs

A big Tyrannosaurus-rex that is as red as the sun
A beautiful pterodactyl flying across a river
A strong triceratops charging at a tree.

Jakob Stove (7)
Staveley Primary School

My Brother

My brother is mean, mad about bikes and sleeps on the sofa.
He would spend the whole time sleeping.
He gobbles his food in one whole gulp.
He plays on his bike.
He does not lurk around very much. He goes on the computer.
But he is my brother, so what's wrong with that?
Great gusts of wind pull him in the night air and out onto his bike.

Daisy Barker (7)
Staveley Primary School

In The Jungle

In the jungle there will be . . .
A monkey climbing up a tree
An alligator in a cascading river
An elephant firing large coconuts.

In the jungle there will be . . .
A toucan swallowing down a bee
A lion gobbling down a deer
A gorilla burping horrendously!

Caleb McLellan (8)
Staveley Primary School

My Big Sister

My big sister is worse than kissing
Because she annoys me
If you're not quick enough to escape she will seal the doors
She will lock the windows
She will get out a microphone
Then the worst bit of all . . .
She sings!

Joseph Skelding (8)
Staveley Primary School

Being Off School

O n holiday somewhere out of the country
F riend's birthday party
F riends help you when you hurt yourself in the swimming pool
    They take you home and tell your parents what has happened
S omeone is ill that you know
C atching fish for tea
H urt yourself on a big rock
O n a trip to buy books for homework
O n a walk to Craggy Wood
L eft your book bag at home.

Jessica Black (7)
Staveley Primary School

My Best Friends

My friends are the best friends in the world,
Nice Nicky, nicest one of all,
Playful Penny playing all the time,
Helpful Holly helping every year, 'Can I help you?'
'No!'
Funny Freddy always making us laugh,
Good and friendly George, friendly every day,
Cheerful Connie cheering all the time,
'Yippee!'

Amy Wood (8)
Staveley Primary School

Hopes And Dreams

Hopes and dreams you hold inside
But will your dreams come true
Like being a wedding bride?
A fear you hate but your sister's great
And seeing is believing
Yet your dreams could come true!

Calum Davison-Bowden (9)
Windermere Junior School

Falling Asleep

The wind blowing round my chimney,
Whistling in my silent room,
Pipes and floorboards creaking madly.
Lying, staring at the blank ceiling,
Dogs barking, cats fighting,
Distant rustling of the trees.
Teenagers making an annoying racket,
Neighbours bellowing angrily,
Ambulance blaring at full blast,
Cars humming quietly,
Gates creaking spookily like a haunted house.
I fall into the land of sleep
Where my dreams are waiting.

William Crisp (10)
Windermere Junior School

Crazy Keith The Koala

Once there was a koala called Keith.
He was crazy, he was lazy,
Just like a daisy!

One day Keith saw a eucalypt leaf.
That leaf it was his favourite nosh
because it was so very posh.
It was lush, green and so easy to be seen,
Cos it was shiny, juicy and green, green, green.

Into his eager tum, tum, tummity tum
Went those lush green leaves- *yum, yum, yummity-yum!*

Emerson Doore (8)
Windermere Junior School

I Wonder

The soft smooth fur of the outstanding bay stallion as I groom him,
I wonder.
I run my hand along his neck, I wonder.
I can feel the sun's rays shining down on me, I wonder.
The grass flicks up into my face, I wonder.
I grasp the reins firmly in my hands waiting for the sound of the bell,
I wonder . . .

I pat my gorgeous, shiny bay stallion on his neck, I wonder
Will I make it through the dressage test before getting disqualified,
I wonder . . .

I tighten the girth before entering the show-jumping ring, I wonder.
Will I make it over the last jump, I wonder . . .

I did a clear round in the 2012 Olympics!

. . . I wonder . . .

Chloe Ackers (10)
Windermere Junior School

Lone Wolf

Split, yellow-moon eyes in silver fur
Scanning dew-dropped grass
Deep growl in endless darkness
Quick-twitching, focussed ears
Dagger-like teeth upon the bloodstained tongue
Quick pace followed by dark shadow
Distant scent of blood from elk
Lone wolf snarling
Claws glint on dead leaves.

Anna McVey (9)
Windermere Junior School

The Beat

I was walking down the street
When I felt the beat in my fingers and toes.
I was walking down the street
When I felt this beat even up my nose.
I was flapping
I was smacking
I was doing the dance
But I couldn't get this rhythm out of my pants!
This super-duper condra zapper
Melody rapper
Orange napper
Music tapper
Tum-tum slapper . . .

Was . . . the . . . beat!

Jessica Irwin (11)
Windermere Junior School

Bedtime Scare

Mum comes up the stairs,
Tucks you into your duvet cover.
While you hug your teddy bears,
She tries to find your little brother,

The light goes out,
The floorboards creak.
You toss and turn,
But you still can't sleep.

Your spine's a-tingling,
You want your mother.
A scuttle, a creak, an open door . . .
And there's your furious monster brother!

Rebekah Booth (11)
Windermere Junior School

The Ages Of School

I started school at the age of four
I was ever so nervous walking through the door

When I was five
I started to strive

Turning six
I learnt to mix

My confidence had grown by the age of seven
I really felt, I was in Heaven

Now I'm eight
Everything is great!

Soon to be nine
I hope I'll be fine

Next year the big ten!
We may go to see Big Ben!

I move to big school on turning eleven
I hope my house group will be 'Leven'

When I turn twelve
Into my studies I will delve

I'll reach thirteen without making a noise
I'm not looking forward to all those boys!

By fourteen I hope I'm doing well
But I'll still listen out for the school bell!

At fifteen I'll be a nervous wreck
The exams are looming - oh heck!

At sixteen I find I've done really well
'All top grades in my results,' I yell

Turning seventeen, I start to drive
One year left, I hope I survive!

It's A Levels now and I'm really worried
I partied hard but never studied!
My future now looks very dire
Ah . . . only forty-two years 'til I retire!

Hannah Thomas (8)
Windermere Junior School

Unfair!

Imagine having no food,
Nor water, with shops pushing and rude,
Imagine the hunger affecting your senses,
Having to kill the cow within your fences

Imagine when it's stopped raining,
The disappointment is almost paining.
Feeling the heat
On your feet,
Whilst look for veg
Or a fruit hedge.

Not having any money,
Some may find it funny.
We wouldn't like it,
Not enough to keep us fit.
I think it's not fair
So now it's time for us all to share.

Bridey Callingham (11)
Windermere Junior School

Oh, What A Silly Billy

There was a young dog called Billy
Who was being terribly silly.
He looked for a bone
But found a stone.
I went for a walk
He thought he could talk.
Oh what a silly Billy.
I rustled the leaves
And he sneezed.
I threw him a stick
And he came back with a brick.
Oh what a silly Billy!

Ellie-Cesca Williams (8)
Windermere Junior School

Senses

I would love to run round Saturn's rings on a dark, twinkling night.

I would love to ride on the back of a wild tiger and glide through the jungle.

To gather the sweet and creamy stripes of the rainbow in my hands and feel the welcoming rush through my body, would be amazing.

I would love to smell the aroma of the scorching sun as I stand at a point where I can see everything.

To smell the reflection of a glistening crystal would be breathtaking.

I would love to savour the rich scent of a summer's day and newly cut grass.

To taste the exotic sensation of a firework spark landing on my tongue would be phenomenal.

I would love to hear the rush of a meteorite speeding past me.

To hear the sound of a black hole absorbing time and space would be thrilling.

I would love to see the joy in a child's eyes opening her first Christmas present.

Colleen Sheehan (11)
Windermere Junior School

Falling To Sleep

Silent muttering, doors slamming,
Smell of autumn is appearing,
Whispering from downstairs,
Out in the night, owls hoot,
Smash! Smash!
Raindrops on roofs like breaking glass,
A floating moon rising from the dead,
People echo loud and clear in the diamond sky,
Smoky smells as if a fire is lit,
Thick sounds of hounds loudly screaming in my ears,
Falling into a deep sleep, my memories come to life.

Mhairi Callingham (9)
Windermere Junior School

A Shepherd's Story

Cold, shivering, sitting on top of the hill,
Sheep grazing on the nourished green grass,
Only sound is wolves howling to their pack,
Bright light appears, blinding me,
Amazing sight of angels singing 'Glory to God',
Sacred Gabriel talking to us,
Angels disappear in a split second,
North Star appears with a heavenly light,
Relief, happiness and fear at the Christmas message,
Rushing to Bethlehem as fast as possible,
Reaching out to the stable, almost there,
Finally at our destination, like a bird migrating,
What a fantastic sight!

Rory Noon (10)
Windermere Junior School

The Wolf

The wolf howls on the windy night,
Giving the animals a terrible fright.
It huffs and puffs as it stalks its prey,
It doesn't eat for another day.

So if you see it, let it be,
As a treat for it . . . is you and me!

Luke Williams (9)
Windermere Junior School

Summer

S unshine falling on a brand new day.
U mbrella up on a rainy day.
M aking noises on the ground.
M ushy marshmallows by the campfire.
E verlasting sunny skies.
R eporting summer in old photos.

Chelsea Louise Walker (11)
Windermere Junior School

Winter Snow

When the snow is lying deep,
When the fields have gone to sleep,
When red roses turn to white,
And frosty stars bejewel the night,
The summer's streams turn to ice,
A frosty snowball warms the heart of mice,
Cosy, cosy up to your head,
Sleeping tight in your bed!

Hannah Clark (11)
Windermere Junior School

The Jigsaw Bird

I love to see the jigsaw bird flying upside down,
It sings a song that sounds all wrong,
And wears a dressing gown.

I love to see the sawjig bird,
Flying downside up,
It feeds on chips and concrete mix,
And drinks them from a cup.

Jennifer Holden (10)
Windermere Junior School

The Wild

Lions and tigers, buffaloes and bears,
Rabbits and weasels, stoats and hares,
Fish and whales, slugs and snails,
Some with feet, some with tails,
Dogs and hogs, cats wearing hats!
All the animals of the world!

Yasmin Wright (10)
Windermere Junior School

Young Writers Information

We hope you have enjoyed reading this book - and that you will continue to enjoy it in the coming years.

If you like reading and writing poetry drop us a line, or give us a call, and we'll send you a free information pack.

Alternatively if you would like to order further copies of this book or any of our other titles, then please give us a call or log onto our website at www.youngwriters.co.uk

Young Writers Information
Remus House
Coltsfoot Drive
Peterborough
PE2 9JX

(01733) 890066